FINISH LINE

Mathematics

for the Common Core State Standards

Continental

ISBN 978-0-8454-6764-0

Table of Contents

Welcome to Finish Line Mathematics for the Common Core State Standards

About This Book

Finish Line Mathematics for the Common Core State Standards will help you prepare for math tests. Each year in math class, you learn new skills and ideas. This book focuses on the math skills and ideas that are the most important for each grade. It is important to master the concepts you learn each year because mathematical ideas and skills build on each other. The things you learn this year will help you understand and master the skills you will learn next year.

This book has units of related lessons. Each lesson concentrates on one main math idea. The lesson reviews things you have learned in math class. It provides explanations and examples. Along the side of each lesson page are reminders to help you recall what you learned in earlier grades.

After the lesson come three pages of practice problems. The problems are the same kinds you find on most math tests. The first page has multiple-choice, or selected-response, problems. Each item has four answers to choose from, and you must select the best answer. At the top of the page is a sample problem with a box beneath it that explains how to find the answer. Then there are a number of problems for you to do on your own.

Constructed-response, or short-answer, items are on the next page. You must answer these items using your own words. Usually, you will need to show your work or write an explanation of your answer in these items. This type of problem helps you demonstrate that you know how to do operations and carry out procedures. They also show that you understand the skill. Again, the first item is a sample and its answer is explained. You will complete the rest of the items by yourself.

The last page has one or two extended-response problems. These items are like the short writing items, but they have more parts and are often a little harder. The first part may ask you to solve a problem and show your work. The second may ask you to explain how you found your answer or why it is correct. This item has a hint to point you in the right direction.

At the end of each unit is a review section. The problems in it cover all the different skills and ideas in the lessons of that unit. The review contains multiple-choice, constructed-response, and extended-response items.

A practice test and a glossary appear at the end of the book. The practice test gives you a chance to try out what you've learned. You will need to use all the skills you have reviewed and practiced in the book on the practice test. The glossary lists important words and terms along with their definitions to help you remember them.

The Goals of Learning Math

Math is everywhere in the world around you. You use math more than you probably realize to help you understand and make sense of that world. But what does it mean to be good at math?

To be good at math, you need to practice certain habits. And you need the right attitude.

- You make sense of problems and do not give up in solving them. You make sure you understand the problem before you try to solve it. You form a plan and then carry out that plan to find an answer. Along the way, you ask yourself if what you are doing makes sense. And if you do not figure out the answer on the first try, you try another way.

- You think about numbers using symbols. You can think about a real-life situation as numbers and operations.

- You draw conclusions about situations and support them with proof. You use what you know about numbers and operations to provide reasons for your conclusions and predictions. When you read or hear someone else's explanation, you think about it and decide if it makes sense. You ask questions that help you better understand the ideas.

- You model with mathematics. You represent real-life problems with a drawing or diagram, a graph, or an equation. You decide if your model makes sense.

- You use the right tools at the right time. You know how to use rulers, protractors, calculators, and other tools. More importantly, you know when to use them.

- You are careful and accurate in your work. You calculate correctly and label answers. You use the correct symbols and definitions. You choose exactly the right words for your explanations and descriptions.

- You look for structure in math. You see how different parts of math are related or connected. You can use an idea you already know to help you understand a new idea. You make connections between things you have already learned and new ideas.

- You look for the patterns in math. When you see the patterns, you can find shortcuts to use that still lead you to the correct answer. You are able to decide if your shortcut worked or not.

These habits help you master new mathematical ideas so that you can remember and use them. All of these habits will make math easier to understand and to do. And that will make it a great tool to use in your everyday life!

Exponents and Radicals

UNIT 1

● **Lesson 1 Exponents** reviews what an integer exponent is and how to evaluate numbers with these exponents.

● **Lesson 2 Laws of Exponents** reviews the rules that show how to multiply and divide numbers with exponents.

● **Lesson 3 Scientific Notation** reviews how to express very small and very large quantities using exponential powers of 10.

● **Lesson 4 Operations with Scientific Notation** reviews how to use all four operations to solve problems involving scientific notation.

● **Lesson 5 Radicals** reviews what a square root and a cube root are and how to find the values of such numbers.

Exponents

8.EE.1

Read 5^3 as "5 to the 3rd power." It means the number 5 is a factor 3 times.

Numbers with negative exponents can also represent repeated division.

$$4^{-2} = 1 \div 4 \div 4$$

Always use parentheses around a base that is negative.

$$(-2)^4 \neq -2^4$$
$$(-2)^4 = -2 \cdot -2 \cdot -2 \cdot -2 = 16$$
$$-2^4 = -(2 \cdot 2 \cdot 2 \cdot 2) = -16$$

A number, *n*, with an exponent of 1 equals *n*.

$$8^1 = 8 \quad (-3)^1 = -3$$
$$\left(\tfrac{2}{5}\right)^1 = \tfrac{2}{5}$$

A number, *n*, with an exponent of 0 equals 1.

$$8^0 = 1 \quad (-3)^0 = 1$$
$$\left(\tfrac{2}{5}\right)^0 = 1$$

When a number is multiplied by itself several times, it is written in **exponential form.** The number being multiplied is called the **base.** The **exponent** shows the number of times it multiplies itself.

$5^3 \leftarrow$ Exponent $\qquad 5^3 = 5 \cdot 5 \cdot 5$
$\uparrow$
Base $\qquad\qquad\qquad\qquad$ 5 multiplies itself 3 times.

Some numbers have negative exponents. These numbers can be rewritten with positive exponents in the denominator of a fraction.

$$4^{-2} = \tfrac{1}{4^2} = \left(\tfrac{1}{4}\right)^2 \qquad\qquad \left(\tfrac{1}{4}\right)^2 = \tfrac{1}{4} \cdot \tfrac{1}{4}$$

4^{-2} is the same as multiplying $\tfrac{1}{4}$ by itself 2 times.

Multiplication is used to find the value of a number in exponential form.

What is the value of 7^4?

In 7^4, the base is 7. The exponent is 4.

Multiply the base by itself 4 times.

$$7^4 = 7 \cdot 7 \cdot 7 \cdot 7 = 2,401$$

What is the value of 6^{-3}?

In 6^{-3}, the base is 6. The exponent is –3.

Rewrite the number as a fraction with a positive exponent.

$$6^{-3} = \tfrac{1}{6^3} = \left(\tfrac{1}{6}\right)^3$$

Now the base is $\tfrac{1}{6}$ and the exponent is 3.

Multiply the base by itself 3 times.

$$6^{-3} = \tfrac{1}{6} \cdot \tfrac{1}{6} \cdot \tfrac{1}{6} = \tfrac{1}{216}$$

SAMPLE What is the value of -5^2?

 A -25 **B** -10 **C** $\frac{1}{25}$ **D** 25

> The correct answer is A. The base is positive 5. The exponent is 2. The negative in front of the base means the answer will be negative. So, $-5^2 = -(5 \cdot 5) = -25$.

1 Which expression is equivalent to 5^4?

 A 54 **C** $5 \cdot 5 \cdot 5 \cdot 5$

 B $5 \cdot 4$ **D** $4 \cdot 4 \cdot 4 \cdot 4 \cdot 4$

2 What is the value of $(-7)^0$?

 A -7 **C** $\frac{1}{7}$

 B 0 **D** 1

3 Which expression is equivalent to the one shown below?

$$(-3) \cdot (-3) \cdot (-3) \cdot (-3) \cdot (-3)$$

 A -3^5 **C** 3^{-5}

 B $(-3)^5$ **D** $(-3)^{-5}$

4 What is the value of 2^5?

 A 10 **C** 25

 B 20 **D** 32

5 What is the value of 10^{-3}?

 A $-1{,}000$ **C** $\frac{1}{30}$

 B -30 **D** $\frac{1}{1{,}000}$

6 What is the value of $(-3)^2$?

 A 9 **C** $\frac{1}{9}$

 B $\frac{1}{6}$ **D** -6

7 The volume of a cube with a side length of s is given by the formula $V = s^3$. What is the volume, in cubic inches, of a cube with a side length of 8 inches?

 A 24 **C** 512

 B 192 **D** $6{,}561$

8 Which expression has the greatest value?

 A 8^{-6} **C** 50^0

 B $(-3)^4$ **D** -125^1

9 Which equation is true?

 A $(-5)^0 = -5$

 B $\frac{1}{8} \cdot \frac{1}{8} = 8 \div 8$

 C $\frac{1}{4} \cdot \frac{1}{4} \cdot \frac{1}{4} = 1 \div 4 \div 4 \div 4$

 D $6^{-4} = (-6) \cdot (-6) \cdot (-6) \cdot (-6)$

SAMPLE Taylor wrote the equation below.

$$(-2)^n = 1$$

What must be the value of n?

Answer _____

 Any base number that has 0 for an exponent will equal 1. Since the equation is equal to 1, the exponent n must be 0.

10 What is the value of $\left(\frac{3}{5}\right)^1$?

Answer _____

11 Are the expressions 5^2 and 2^5 equivalent? Explain how you know.

_____

_____

12 Write an expression using multiplication and an expression using division that are equivalent to 7^{-3}.

Multiplication _____

Division _____

13 Are the expressions $(-3)^3$ and -3^3 equivalent? Explain how you know.

_____

_____

14 Ariel wrote these expressions.

$$6^3 \qquad 3^5 \qquad 10^2$$

Part A Write these expressions in order from least to greatest.

Answer _____

Part B Explain how you know your answer is correct

_____

_____

_____

15 Kevin wrote the expression 9^{-2}.

Part A What is the value of this expression?

Answer _____

Part B Is the expression $(-9)^2$ equivalent to 9^{-2}? Explain how you know.

_____

_____

_____

How can you change a negative exponent to a positive exponent?

Laws of Exponents

8.EE.1

To combine exponential expressions with the same base, combine the exponents only. The base stays the same.

To change a negative exponent to a positive exponent, rewrite the number as a fraction with a positive exponent.

$$2^{-3} = \frac{1}{2^3}$$

Follow the rules for adding, subtracting, and multiplying integers when combining exponents.

Laws of exponents can be used to combine exponential expressions with the same base.

To multiply exponential expressions, add the exponents.

$$n^a \cdot n^b = n^{(a + b)} \qquad 2^4 \cdot 2^3 = 2^{(4 + 3)} = 2^7$$

To divide exponential expressions, subtract the exponents.

$$n^a \div n^b = n^{(a - b)} \qquad 5^3 \div 5^{-2} = 5^{(3 - (-2))} = 5^5$$

To raise an exponential expression to a power, multiply the exponents.

$$(n^a)^b = n^{(a \cdot b)} \qquad (3^{-4})^2 = 3^{(-4 \cdot 2)} = 3^{-8} = \frac{1}{3^8}$$

What is the value of $\left(\frac{2^{-3} \cdot 2^5}{2^4}\right)^2$?

First, add the exponents to multiply the expressions in the numerator of the fraction.

$$\left(\frac{2^{-3} \cdot 2^5}{2^4}\right)^2 = \left(\frac{2^{(-3 + 5)}}{2^4}\right)^2 = \left(\frac{2^2}{2^4}\right)^2$$

Next, subtract the exponents to divide the expressions inside parentheses.

$$\left(\frac{2^2}{2^4}\right) = (2^{(2 - 4)})^2 = (2^{-2})^2$$

Then multiply the exponents to raise the expression to the power 2.

$$(2^{-2})^2 = 2^{(-2 \cdot 2)} = 2^{-4}$$

Finally, rewrite the expression using a positive exponent and evaluate.

$$2^{-4} = \frac{1}{2^4} = \frac{1}{16}, \text{ so } \left(\frac{2^{-3} \cdot 2^5}{2^4}\right)^2 = \frac{1}{16}$$

SAMPLE What is the value of $(-4)^6 \div (-4)^3$?

    A -64   **B** -16   **C** 16   **D** 64

> The correct answer is A. Two exponential expressions with the same base, –4, are being divided. The law of exponents says you can subtract the exponents: $(-4)^{(6-3)} = (-4)^3$. Then evaluate: $(-4)(-4)(-4) = -64$.

1 Which expression is equivalent to $8^3 \cdot 8^5$?

  A 8^8 **C** 64^8

  B 8^{15} **D** 64^{15}

2 What is the value of $(2^3)^{-2}$?

  A -64   **C** $\frac{1}{64}$

  B -12   **D** 2

3 Simplify the expression below.

$$\frac{(-6)^8}{(-6)^2}$$

  A 6^4 **C** $(-6)^4$

  B 6^6 **D** $(-6)^6$

4 What is the value of $3^4 \cdot 3^{-7}$?

  A -84   **C** $\frac{1}{9}$

  B -9   **D** $\frac{1}{27}$

5 What is the value of this expression?

$$4^{-1} \cdot 4^6 \div 4^3$$

  A 16   **C** $\frac{1}{4}$

  B 4   **D** $\frac{1}{16}$

6 Simplify the expression below.

$$\frac{(10^{-6})^{-2}}{10^{-4}}$$

  A $\frac{1}{10^3}$ **C** 10^8

  B $\frac{1}{10^2}$ **D** 10^{16}

7 What is the value of this expression?

$$\frac{5^0 \cdot 5^4}{5^3 \cdot 5^1}$$

  A 0   **C** 5

  B 1   **D** 25

SAMPLE The two expressions below have the same value.

$$\frac{2^6}{2^2} \qquad 2^n \cdot 2^5$$

What is the value of n?

Answer _____

First simplify each expression:

$$\frac{2^6}{2^2} = 2^{(6-2)} = 2^4 \qquad 2^n \cdot 2^5 = 2^{(n+5)} = 2^4$$

The exponents $n + 5$ and 4 are the same, so $n + 5 = 4$, and $n = -1$.

8 Simplify $(4^3 \cdot 4^{-5})^4$. Write your answer using a positive exponent.

Answer _____

9 What is the value of $2^3 \cdot \frac{2^4}{2^1}$? Show your work.

Answer _____

10 Courtney thinks the value of $\frac{(3^{-2})^2}{3^{-3}}$ is $\frac{1}{3}$. Is she correct? Explain how you know.

_____

_____

11 Michael wrote this expression.

$$4^6 \cdot 4^{-3} \cdot 4^1$$

Part A What is the value of the expression?

Answer _____

Part B Write an exponential expression using division that has the same value as the one Michael wrote.

Answer _____

12 Look at this expression.

$$\left(\frac{3^0}{3^2}\right)^{-1}$$

Part A What is the value of this expression? Show your work.

What is the value of any number raised to the 0 power?

Answer _____

Part B Troy found the value of this expression by first subtracting the exponents of the numbers inside the parentheses. Marni found the value of the expression by first multiplying each term of the fraction by the exponent –1. If all their math work is correct, will Troy and Marni get the same value? Explain how you know.

_____

_____

_____

A number in scientific notation should always have *only* one digit to the left of the decimal point.

The decimal point for an integer is to the right of its ones place.

$43 = 43.0 \quad -6 = -6.0$

The zeros after the last digit in a decimal can be dropped without changing the value of the number.

$4.5080000 = 4.508$

A number in scientific notation is very large if the power of 10 is positive.

A number in scientific notation is very small if the power of 10 is negative.

In scientific notation, $75 = 7.5 \times 10^1$. The exponent, 1, increases the original exponent by 1, from −3 to −2.

Scientific notation can be used to write very large or very small numbers. In scientific notation, a number greater than or equal to 1 and less than 10 is multiplied by a power of 10.

You can move the decimal point in numbers to change them from standard form to scientific notation and from scientific notation to standard form.

Write the number 45,080,000 in scientific notation.

Place a decimal point to the right of the first digit to make a number greater than or equal to 1 and less than 10.

$$45,080,000 \rightarrow 4.5080000 = 4.508$$

Multiply this number by a power of 10. The exponent is equal to the number of places the decimal point moved. The decimal point moved 7 places, so the power is 10^7.

$$45,080,000 = 4.508 \times 10^7$$

Write the number 3.6025×10^{-5} in standard form.

Move the decimal point the same number of places as the number in the exponent. Then drop the power of 10. The negative exponent means the number is very small and the decimal point moves to the left.

$$3.6025 \times 10^{-5} = 0.000036025$$

You can estimate amounts using scientific notation.

A penny is about 1.54×10^{-3} meter thick. A roll of coins contains 50 pennies. Estimate the thickness of the roll of coins.

Round the decimal part 1.54 to 1.5. Then multiply by 50 to get 75. The thickness of the roll of coins is about 75×10^{-3} meter. Numbers in scientific notation can have only one digit to the left of the decimal point, so $75 \times 10^{-3} = 7.5 \times 10^{-2}$.

A roll of coins is about 7.5×10^{-2} meter thick.

SAMPLE The Great Lakes have a water area of about 2.44×10^5 square kilometers. One of them, Lake Huron, has a water area of about 6.0×10^4 square kilometers. What approximate fraction of the total water area of the Great Lakes does Lake Huron represent?

A $\frac{1}{6}$ B $\frac{1}{5}$ C $\frac{1}{4}$ D $\frac{1}{3}$

The correct answer is C. First change each number from scientific notation to standard form: $2.44 \times 10^5 = 244{,}000$ and $6.0 \times 10^4 = 60{,}000$. Round 244,000 to a compatible number: 240,000. Then divide this into 60,000: $60{,}000 \div 240{,}000 = 0.25 = \frac{1}{4}$. Lake Huron represents $\frac{1}{4}$ of the total water area.

1 Which number is written in correct scientific notation?

A 5,000   C 5.0×10^{-4}

B 0.5×10^2 D 50×10^5

2 About 4.0×10^6 people live in Washington, D.C. How is this number written in standard form?

A 0.000004   C 400,000

B 0.0000004   D 4,000,000

3 How is 28,301,000,000 written in scientific notation?

A 2.8301×10^9 C 28.301×10^9

B 2.8301×10^{10} D 28.301×10^{10}

4 An ant can lift a total of 3.3×10^{-3} kilogram. What is this number written in standard form?

A 0.0033   C 3,300

B 0.00033   D 33,000

5 The land area of Connecticut is about 4.8×10^3 square miles. The land area of New Mexico is about 1.2×10^5 square miles. About how many times greater is the land area of New Mexico than the land area of Connecticut?

A 4   C 25

B 20   D 40

6 How is 0.980063 written in scientific notation?

A 9.863×10^{-1} C 9.80063×10^{-1}

B 9.863×10^{-5} D 9.80063×10^{-5}

7 The diameter of Venus is approximately 1.2×10^4 kilometers wide. The diameter of Jupiter is about 12 times wider than this. Which is the best estimate for the width of the diameter of Jupiter?

A 1.44×10^4 C 1.2×10^{16}

B 1.44×10^5 D 1.2×10^{48}

SAMPLE There are one billion nanoseconds in one second. Write the number of nanoseconds in one second using scientific notation.

Answer _____

First, write one billion as a number in standard form. One billion is 1,000,000,000. Then write this number in scientific notation. The decimal point goes directly after the 1. Since the decimal point is moved 9 places, the number is 1.0×10^9.

8 A company made $13,450,000 in sales last year. Write this number in scientific notation.

Answer _____

9 Write the number 5.93×10^{-6} in standard form.

Answer _____

10 The mass of a proton is about 2,000 times greater than the mass of an electron. The mass of an electron is about 9.0×10^{-31} kilogram. What is the approximate mass, in kilograms, of a proton? Show your work.

Answer _____

11 A skyscraper is 2.0×10^4 inches tall. A bug is 2.0×10^{-2} inch tall. How many times greater is the height of the skyscraper than the height of the bug? Show your work.

Answer _____

UNIT 1 ▓▓▓▓▓▓▓▓▓▓▓▓▓▓▓▓▓▓▓▓▓▓▓▓▓▓▓▓▓▓▓▓▓▓▓▓▓▓▓
Exponents and Radicals

12 The weights, in ounces, of different animals are shown in the table below.

WEIGHT OF ANIMALS

Animal	Weight (ounces)
Elephant	2.28×10^5
Cat	1.92×10^2
Mouse	7.3×10^{-1}
Zebra	9.6×10^3

Part A Approximately how many times heavier is an elephant than a mouse?

It may help to change the numbers in scientific notation to standard form and use compatible numbers.

Answer _____

Part B Explain how you found your answer.

_____

_____

_____

_____

Operations with Scientific Notation

8.EE.4

It is easier to adjust the smaller number to have the same power of 10 as the larger number.

To change a number in scientific notation to have a larger power of 10, follow these steps:

1. Find n, the number the power of 10 increases by.

2. Move the decimal point to the left n places.

Remember to add exponents when multiplying powers of 10 and subtract exponents when dividing powers of 10.

The **commutative property** says you can add or multiply numbers in any order and the result will be the same.

$$a + b = b + a$$
$$3 + 8 = 8 + 3$$
$$a \times b = b \times a$$
$$5 \times 7 = 7 \times 5$$

Numbers in scientific notation can be combined using basic operations.

To add or subtract, rewrite the problem so that both numbers have the same power of 10.

Find the sum.

$$4.75 \times 10^8 + 9.1 \times 10^6$$

Rewrite 9.1×10^6 so 10 is to the 8th power: $9.1 \times 10^6 = 0.091 \times 10^8$

Add the decimal numbers. The power of 10 stays the same.

$$4.75 \times 10^8 + 0.091 \times 10^8 = (4.75 + 0.091) \times 10^8$$
$$= 4.841 \times 10^8$$

So, $4.75 \times 10^8 + 9.1 \times 10^6 = 4.841 \times 10^8$.

To multiply or divide, first multiply or divide the decimal numbers. Then multiply or divide the powers of 10.

Find the product.

$$(5.5 \times 10^4)(3.0 \times 10^5)$$

Rewrite the problem using the commutative property.

$$(5.5 \times 10^4)(3.0 \times 10^5) = (5.5 \times 3.0)(10^4 \times 10^5)$$

Multiply the decimal numbers. Then multiply the powers of 10.

$$(5.5 \times 3.0)(10^4 \times 10^5) = 16.5 \times 10^{4 + 5}$$
$$= 16.5 \times 10^9$$

Write the result in proper scientific notation.

$$16.5 \times 10^9 = 1.65 \times 10^{10}$$

So, $(5.5 \times 10^4)(3.0 \times 10^5) = 1.65 \times 10^{10}$.

SAMPLE The temperature at the surface of the sun is approximately 1.0×10^4 degrees Fahrenheit. The temperature at its center is approximately 2.7×10^7 degrees Fahrenheit. About how many times greater is the temperature at the center of the sun than at its surface?

    A $2.7 \times 10^{1.75}$ **B** 2.7×10^3 **C** 2.7×10^{11} **D** 2.7×10^{28}

The correct answer is B. Division is used to determine how many times greater one number is than another. Write a division expression: $(2.7 \times 10^7) \div (1.0 \times 10^4)$. Divide the decimal numbers: $2.7 \div 1.0 = 2.7$. Then divide the powers of 10: $10^7 \div 10^4 = 10^{7-4} = 10^3$. So, $(2.7 \times 10^7) \div (1.0 \times 10^4) = 2.7 \times 10^3$.

1 Rob correctly combined 8.4×10^5 and 6.24×10^6 and got 7.08×10^6. What operation did he use?

    A addition   **C** multiplication

    B subtraction   **D** division

2 The area of North America is about 9.365×10^6 square miles. The area of South America is about 6.88×10^6 square miles. What is the approximate total area, in square miles, of both North and South America?

    A 1.6245×10^6 **C** 1.6245×10^{12}

    B 1.6245×10^7 **D** 1.6245×10^{13}

3 What is $12.5 - (3.3 \times 10^{-3})$?

    A 9.2×10^3 **C** 1.24967×10^1

    B 9.2×10^{-3} **D** 1.24967×10^{-1}

4 Television ratings show 1.7×10^7 people watched show X and 8.0×10^5 people watched show Y. Which statement is true?

    A 1.62×10^2 more people watched X.

    B 1.62×10^7 more people watched X.

    C 6.3×10^2 more people watched Y.

    D 6.3×10^5 more people watched Y.

5 A light-year is the distance light travels in a year. One light-year is about 5.88×10^{12} miles. The sun is about 1.6×10^{-5} light-years from Earth. About how many miles is the sun from Earth?

    A 4.28×10^{17} **C** 7.48×10^7

    B 3.675×10^{17} **D** 9.408×10^7

6 A scale drawing of an insect is 7.2 cm long. The actual length of the insect is 3.6×10^{-2} cm. How many times smaller is the actual length compared to the scale drawing?

    A 20   **C** 200

    B 50   **D** 500

SAMPLE One megabyte is approximately 1.05×10^6 bytes. One gigabyte is 1.024×10^3 megabytes. Approximately how many bytes are in one gigabyte?

Answer _____

Multiply to find the number of bytes in one gigabyte: $(1.05 \times 10^6)(1.024 \times 10^3) = (1.05 \times 1.024)(10^6 \times 10^3) = 1.0752 \times 10^{6+3} = 1.0752 \times 10^9$. So, one gigabyte is about 1.0752×10^9 bytes.

7 Find the quotient. Write your answer in proper scientific notation.

$$2.05 \times 10^8 \div 8.2 \times 10^4$$

Answer _____

8 The length of a rectangle is 1.2×10^{-4} kilometer. The width of the rectangle is 6.25×10^{-5} kilometer. What is the area, in square kilometers, of this rectangle? Show your work.

Answer _____

9 Katherine found the difference of $7.5 \times 10^{11} - 4.3 \times 10^8$ as 3.2×10^3. Explain whether or not Katherine is correct.

_____

_____

_____

_____

10 The approximate densities of some chemical elements are shown in the table below.

DENSITY OF ELEMENTS

Element	Density (kilograms per cubic centimeter)
Calcium	1.5×10^{-3}
Gold	1.932×10^{-2}
Silver	1.05×10^{-2}
Sodium	9.71×10^{-4}

Part A What is the density, in kilograms per cubic centimeter, of gold and sodium together? Show your work.

Answer _____

Part B How many times greater is the density of silver than of calcium? Explain how you know.

_____

_____

_____

_____

Which operation would you use to find how many times greater one number is than another?

Radicals

8.EE.2

A number multiplied by itself is a **squared** number.

$$4^2 = 4 \times 4 = 16$$

The **radical** symbol $\sqrt{\ }$ is used to show a square root. The number under the radical is called the **radicand**.

$$\sqrt{25} \leftarrow \text{Radicand}$$

The first ten perfect squares are

$1^2 = 1$	$6^2 = 36$
$2^2 = 4$	$7^2 = 49$
$3^2 = 9$	$8^2 = 64$
$4^2 = 16$	$9^2 = 81$
$5^2 = 25$	$10^2 = 100$

A number multiplied by itself twice is a **cubed** number.

$$4^3 = 4 \times 4 \times 4 = 64$$

The first five perfect cubes are

$$1^3 = 1$$
$$2^3 = 8$$
$$3^3 = 27$$
$$4^3 = 64$$
$$5^3 = 125$$

A **perfect square** is the product of a number and itself. A **square root** is the inverse of a perfect square. The square root of a number x is the number that is squared to equal x.

What is the value of $\sqrt{144}$?

Think: What number squared equals 144?

Since 12^2, or 12×12, equals 144, $\sqrt{144} = 12$.

A **perfect cube** is the product of the same three numbers. The **cube root** of a number x is the number that is cubed to equal x. The symbol $\sqrt[3]{x}$ represents the cubed root of x.

What is $\sqrt[3]{343}$?

Think: What number cubed equals 343?

Since 7^3, or $7 \times 7 \times 7$ equals 343, $\sqrt[3]{343} = 7$.

The square root and the cube root of a number are **not** always whole numbers.

Between what two consecutive whole numbers is $\sqrt{50}$?

Find the closest perfect squares greater and less than 50.

$$7^2 = 49 \text{ and } 8^2 = 64$$

50 is between 49 and 64, so $\sqrt{50}$ is between 7 and 8. Since 50 is closer to 49 than 64, $\sqrt{50}$ is closer to 7 than 8.

Between what two consecutive whole numbers is $\sqrt[3]{100}$?

Find the closest perfect cubes greater and less than 100.

$$4^3 = 64 \text{ and } 5^3 = 125$$

100 is between 64 and 125, so $\sqrt[3]{100}$ is between 4 and 5.

24

UNIT 1 ::
Exponents and Radicals

SAMPLE Which value is closest to $\sqrt[3]{200}$?

    A 5.8   **B** 6.7   **C** 10.2   **D** 14.1

> The correct answer is A. Find cubes of numbers that are just under and just over 200. Since $5^3 = 125$ and $6^3 = 216$, $\sqrt[3]{200}$ is between 5 and 6. Since 200 is closer to 216 than it is to 125, $\sqrt[3]{200}$ is closer to 6 than it is to 5. A reasonable estimate for $\sqrt[3]{200}$ is 5.8.

1 Which of these numbers is a perfect square?

  A 200   **C** 600

  B 400   **D** 800

2 The area of a square picture is 64 square inches. What is the length of the picture?

  A 4 inches   **C** 8 inches

  B 6 inches   **D** 10 inches

3 Which of the following numbers is **not** a perfect cube?

  A 27   **C** 512

  B 125   **D** 900

4 Between what two consecutive whole numbers is $\sqrt{75}$?

  A 5 and 6   **C** 7 and 8

  B 6 and 7   **D** 8 and 9

5 What is the perimeter of the triangle below?

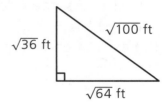

  A 14 ft   **C** 100 ft

  B 24 ft   **D** 200 ft

6 Which value is closest to $\sqrt[3]{42}$?

  A 3.5   **C** 5.2

  B 4.2   **D** 6.5

7 Which radical is closest in value to 7.5?

  A $\sqrt{45}$ **C** $\sqrt{65}$

  B $\sqrt{55}$ **D** $\sqrt{75}$

8 Preeti wrote the equation below.

$$n^3 = 81$$

Which number is closest in value to n?

  A 4.3   **C** 8.1

  B 6.4   **D** 9.0

SAMPLE The volume of a cube with a side length of s is s^3 cubic units. The volume of the cube below is 512 cubic centimeters.

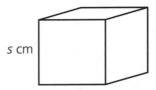

s cm

What is the area, in square centimeters, of each side of the cube?

Answer _____

First find s, the side length of the cube. Since $8^3 = 8 \times 8 \times 8 = 512$, $\sqrt[3]{512} = 8$. The area of each square side on the cube is s^2. So, the area of each side is $8^2 = 64$ square centimeters.

9 The base of a square pyramid has an area of 625 square inches. What is the length, in inches, of each side of the square base?

Answer _____

10 Mateo thinks the cube root of 1,000 is 10. Is he correct? Explain how you know.

_____

_____

11 Between which two consecutive whole numbers is $\sqrt{150}$? Explain how you found your answer.

_____

_____

12 The floor of a square bedroom has an area of 169 square feet.

Part A What is the length, in feet, of each side of the bedroom floor?

Answer _____

Part B The floor of a square family room has an area twice as great as the area of this bedroom floor. Is the length of each side of the family room floor twice as great as the length of each side of the bedroom floor? Explain how you know.

> Find the area of the family room floor. Is this area a perfect square?

_____

_____

_____

13 Alex wants to estimate the value of $\sqrt[3]{120}$.

Part A Between which two consecutive whole numbers is $\sqrt[3]{120}$?

Answer _____

Part B Estimate the value of $\sqrt[3]{120}$ to the nearest tenth. Explain how you know your estimate is correct.

_____

_____

_____

REVIEW

Exponents and Radicals

Read each problem. Circle the letter of the best answer.

1 Which expression is equivalent to 6^5?

   A   65   **C** $6 \cdot 6 \cdot 6 \cdot 6 \cdot 6$

   B $6 \cdot 5$ **D** $5 \cdot 5 \cdot 5 \cdot 5 \cdot 5 \cdot 5$

2 The area of a square dance floor is 196 square feet. What is the length of each side of the dance floor?

   A   14 feet   **C**   18 feet

   B   16 feet   **D**   24 feet

3 A bee's wings can beat about 6.48×10^5 times an hour. How is this number written in standard form?

   A   64,800   **C**   6,480,000

   B   648,000   **D**   64,800,000

4 What is the value of $(3^0)^{-3}$?

   A   –9   **C** $\frac{1}{27}$

   B   0   **D**   1

5 Which number is equivalent to 0.0020635?

   A 2.635×10^{-2} **C** 2.0635×10^{-2}

   B 2.635×10^{-3} **D** 2.0635×10^{-3}

6 About 1.37×10^7 people in South Africa speak English. English is the primary language for about 3.7×10^6 of these people. The rest speak it as a secondary language. About how many speak English as a secondary language?

   A 1.0×10^6 **C** 2.33×10^1

   B 1.0×10^7 **D** 2.33×10^6

7 Which of these equations is true?

   A $3^2 = 3 \cdot 2$

   B $\left(\frac{1}{5}\right)^3 = \frac{1}{5} \div \frac{1}{5} \div \frac{1}{5}$

   C $2^{-4} = \frac{1}{2 \cdot 2 \cdot 2 \cdot 2}$

   D $4^{-3} = (-4) \cdot (-4) \cdot (-4)$

8 The longest bone in the human body averages about 5.05×10^{-1} m in length. The shortest bone averages 2.8×10^{-3} m. About how many times greater is the length of the longest bone than the shortest bone?

   A   200   **C**   2,000

   B   500   **D**   5,000

9 What is the value of $\left(\frac{2}{5}\right)^{-1}$?

Answer _____

10 One year, India produced more than 21,500,000 tons of bananas. How is this number written in scientific notation?

Answer _____

11 Are the expressions $(-2)^4$ and -2^4 equivalent? Explain how you know.

_____

_____

12 Between which two consecutive whole numbers is $\sqrt[3]{300}$?

Answer _____

13 What is the value of the expression $2^6 \cdot 2^{-9}$?

Answer _____

14 What is the value of $95.04 + (6.39 \times 10^3)$? Write your answer in scientific notation.

Answer _____

15 Tia thinks the quotient $(1.2 \times 10^9) \div (4.0 \times 10^3)$ is equal to 3.0×10^5. Explain whether or not Tia is correct.

_____

_____

16 Damian wrote the equation $n^3 = \frac{64}{125}$. What is the value of n?

Answer _____

Read each problem. Write your answer to each part.

17 Mr. Wyler wrote the expression $5^3 \cdot 5^0 \cdot 5^{-5}$.

Part A What is the value of this expression?

Answer ____________

Part B Write an exponential expression using division that is equivalent to the one Mr. Wyler wrote.

Answer ________________________

18 The United States government produced about 10.25 billion pennies one year.

Part A How is 10.25 billion written in scientific notation?

Answer ________________________

Part B That same year, about 3.0×10^7 half-dollars were produced. How many more pennies were produced that year than half-dollars? Explain how you know.

____

____

____

____

● **Lesson 1 Rational Numbers** reviews what a rational number is and what numbers make up the rational numbers.

● **Lesson 2 Irrational Numbers** reviews what an irrational number is, what numbers make up the irrational numbers, and how to find approximate values of irrational numbers.

Rational Numbers

8.NS.1

The **real numbers** are made up of rational numbers and irrational numbers.

Whole numbers include the counting numbers 1, 2, 3, 4, ... and 0.

Integers include whole numbers and their opposites.

A fraction with a numerator that is equal to or greater than the denominator is called an **improper fraction**.

The bar symbol above digits in a decimal is used to show digits that repeat.

$6.828282... = 6.\overline{82}$

Ellipses (...) indicate that a number continues.

A **rational number** is any number that can be written as a fraction. All whole numbers, integers, fractions, improper fractions, and mixed numbers are rational numbers.

Show that each of these numbers is a rational number.

$$0.5 \qquad 6\frac{1}{3} \qquad -13 \qquad 0$$

$0.5 = \frac{1}{2}$, so 0.5 is rational.

$6\frac{1}{3} = \frac{3 \times 6 + 1}{3} = \frac{19}{3}$, which is an improper fraction, so $6\frac{1}{3}$ is rational.

$-13 = -\frac{13}{1}$, so -13 is rational.

$0 = \frac{0}{1}$, so 0 is rational.

Some decimal numbers are rational numbers. A decimal is rational if it terminates or repeats. A **terminating decimal** is a decimal number whose digits end. A **repeating decimal** is a decimal number with digits that repeat in a pattern.

Which of these numbers are rational numbers?

$$-2.75 \qquad 1.\overline{2} \qquad 5.48326... \qquad -8.5333... \qquad 3\frac{2}{9} \qquad 0.010309...$$

-2.75 is a terminating decimal, so it is rational.

$1.\overline{2}$ and -8.5333... are repeating decimals, so they are rational.

$3\frac{2}{9}$ can be written as the improper fraction $\frac{29}{9}$, so it is rational.

5.48326... and 0.010309... are neither terminating nor repeating decimals, so they are **not** rational.

UNIT 2 ▨▨▨▨▨▨▨▨▨▨▨▨▨▨▨▨▨▨▨▨▨▨▨▨▨▨▨▨▨▨▨▨▨▨▨▨▨
Real Numbers

SAMPLE Which of the following is *not* a rational number?

A   -8.5837   B $-3\frac{4}{11}$ C $\frac{31}{5}$ D   5.47838...

> The correct answer is D. A rational number is any number that can be written as a fraction. This includes all fractions, mixed numbers, improper fractions, integers, and terminating or repeating decimals. The decimal number in choice A terminates, a mixed number is in choice B, and an improper fraction is in choice C. All of these are rational numbers. The decimal in choice D does not terminate or repeat, so it cannot be written as a fraction and is not rational.

1 Which type of number is *not* rational?

A   negative integer

B   improper fraction

C   repeating decimal

D   non-terminating decimal

2 Which decimal is rational?

A   -6.12341234...

B   -7.88238274...

C   8.1020030006...

D   9.1526374859...

3 Which statement is true of the numbers $\frac{39}{7}$ and $-0.32\overline{8}$?

A   Only $\frac{39}{7}$ is rational.

B   Only $-0.32\overline{8}$ is rational.

C   Both numbers are rational.

D   Both numbers are not rational.

4 Which of these numbers is *not* rational?

A   -101   C   -2.53545565...

B   913   D   7.42839495236

5 Julius thinks the number $6.\overline{45}$ is rational. Is he correct?

A   Yes, because the decimal repeats.

B   Yes, because the decimal terminates.

C   No, because the number is not a fraction.

D   No, because the number is not an integer.

6 Which equation shows why 0.33... is a rational number?

A   0.33... = 0.33

B   0.33... = $0.\overline{3}$

C   0.33... = $\frac{1}{3}$

D   0.33... = 0.3333...

SAMPLE Tyler wrote these numbers.

$$6\frac{1}{2} \qquad -11 \qquad 0.829 \qquad -4.636363\ldots$$

Which of these numbers are rational?

Answer _____

A rational number is any number that can be written as a fraction. Mixed numbers like $6\frac{1}{2}$, integers like –11, terminating decimals like 0.829, and repeating decimals like –4.636363… can all be written as fractions. So, all are rational.

7 Write a decimal number that is **not** a rational number.

Answer _____

8 Show that 0.357 is a rational number.

_____

_____

9 Gregory thinks –6.9 is not a rational number because it is not a fraction. Is Gregory correct? Explain how you know.

_____

_____

10 Use a calculator to change $\frac{1}{7}$ to a decimal. What kind of decimal is it?

Answer _____

11 Look at this set of numbers.

$$\frac{0}{17} \qquad 0.728283\ldots \qquad -0.555\ldots \qquad \frac{13}{6}$$

$$-1.572735\ldots \qquad 11.875$$

Part A Which of these numbers are **not** rational?

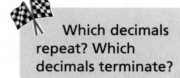

Which decimals repeat? Which decimals terminate?

Answer _____

Part B Explain how you know your answer is correct

_____

_____

_____

12 Cassandra changed $\frac{3}{11}$ to a decimal.

Part A Write the decimal number that is equivalent to $\frac{3}{11}$.

Answer _____

Part B Which type of decimal best describes $\frac{3}{11}$ — terminating, not terminating, repeating, or not repeating? Explain how you know.

_____

_____

_____

Irrational Numbers

8.NS.1, 8.NS.2

Rational numbers and irrational numbers make up the real numbers.

A **non-terminating decimal** is a decimal number whose digits do not end.

A **non-repeating decimal** is a decimal number whose digits do not repeat.

The square root of a number that is not a perfect square is an irrational number.

The square root of a fraction can be written as the square root of the numerator divided by the square root of the denominator.

$$\sqrt{\frac{3}{5}} = \frac{\sqrt{3}}{\sqrt{5}}$$

Common approximations for π are 3.14 and $\frac{22}{7}$.

An **irrational number** is a real number that cannot be written in fraction form. Irrational numbers are decimals that are non-terminating and non-repeating.

Most square roots are irrational numbers. The number pi (π) is also irrational. **Pi** equals the ratio of the circumference of a circle to its diameter. The value of π is always 3.141592654….

Explain whether these numbers are rational or irrational.

$$-3.048476 \qquad 7.124578\ldots \qquad \sqrt{\frac{16}{81}} \qquad \sqrt{10}$$

–3.048476 is a terminating decimal, so it is rational.

7.124578… is a non-terminating and non-repeating decimal, so it is irrational.

$\sqrt{\frac{16}{81}}$ can be written as the square root of the quotient of two perfect squares, $\frac{\sqrt{16}}{\sqrt{81}} = \frac{4}{9}$, so it is rational.

$\sqrt{10}$ is not the square root of a perfect square, so it is irrational.

Rational numbers approximate the value of irrational numbers.

Draw a dot to show the approximate location of $\sqrt{2}$ on this number line.

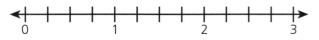

Find the roots of two perfect squares that $\sqrt{2}$ lies between.

$$\sqrt{1} \text{ and } \sqrt{4}$$

$\sqrt{1} = 1$ and $\sqrt{4} = 2$, so the value of $\sqrt{2}$ is between 1 and 2.

Since $\sqrt{2}$ is a little closer to $\sqrt{1}$ than it is to $\sqrt{4}$, a good approximation for $\sqrt{2}$ is 1.4.

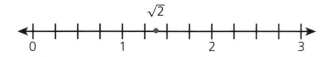

Read each problem. Circle the letter of the best answer.

SAMPLE Which number is closest in value to $\sqrt{3} \cdot \sqrt{11}$?

    A 3.11   **B** 5.61   **C** 9.9   **D** 18.7

> The correct answer is B. Find two consecutive perfect squares that surround 3 and 11. Use these to approximate the values of $\sqrt{3}$ and $\sqrt{11}$. Since 3 is between 1 and 4, $\sqrt{3}$ is between $\sqrt{1}$ and $\sqrt{4}$: $\sqrt{3} \approx 1.7$. Since 11 is between 9 and 16, $\sqrt{11}$ is between $\sqrt{9}$ and $\sqrt{16}$: $\sqrt{11} \approx 3.3$. Multiply the approximate values: $1.7 \times 3.3 = 5.61$.

1 Which of these numbers is irrational?

  A $\frac{2}{9}$ **C** $\sqrt{\frac{2}{9}}$

  B $\frac{25}{4}$ **D** $\sqrt{\frac{25}{4}}$

2 Which statement best explains why –6.048572… is an irrational number?

  A It is negative.

  B It is not a fraction.

  C It is a not a whole number.

  D It is a non-terminating decimal.

3 Which of these numbers lies between 4 and 4.5 on a number line?

  A $\sqrt{13}$ **C** $\sqrt{22}$

  B $\sqrt{17}$ **D** $\sqrt{28}$

4 Which statement is true?

  A $\pi = \frac{22}{7}$ **C** $\sqrt{12} < 3.5$

  B $\pi < 3.14$ **D** $\sqrt{12} > 3.5$

5 Which number line shows the approximate location of $\sqrt{8}$?

A
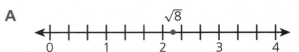

B

C

D

6 Which statement best describes the value of $\sqrt{\pi}$?

  A It is less than 2.

  B It is between 2 and 2.5.

  C It is between 2.5 and 3.

  D It is greater than 3.

SAMPLE Write these numbers in order from least to greatest.

$$\sqrt{90} \qquad 9.24485793\ldots \qquad \pi^2$$

Answer _____

> Find rational approximations for $\sqrt{90}$ and π^2. The number $\sqrt{90}$ is almost directly between $\sqrt{81} = 9$ and $\sqrt{100} = 10$, so $\sqrt{90}$ is approximately 9.5. Since π is approximately 3.14, π^2 is approximately $(3.14)^2 = 9.8596$. The numbers, in order from least to greatest, are $9.24485793\ldots, \sqrt{90}, \pi^2$.

7 Write a number between –7.6 and –7.5 that is irrational.

Answer _____

8 Which of these numbers are irrational?

$$\sqrt{3^3} \qquad 2.634634\ldots \qquad \sqrt{\frac{3}{12}} \qquad -8.63733\ldots$$

Answer _____

9 Place a dot on the number line below to show the approximate location of $-\sqrt{\frac{5}{2}}$.

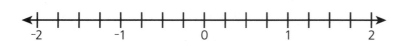

10 Is the number $\sqrt{\frac{4}{10}}$ rational or irrational? Explain how you know.

_____

_____

_____

11 Jessica wrote the numbers in the table below to represent the side lengths of four different squares.

SIDE LENGTHS OF SQUARES

Square	Side Length (in.)
A	6.58333…
B	$\sqrt{41}$
C	2π
D	$6\frac{5}{6}$

Part A Which of these squares have side lengths that are irrational numbers?

Answer _____

Part B List these side lengths in order from least to greatest. Explain how you know your answer is correct.

Find decimal equivalents or approximations for all side lengths. Then compare the decimals.

_____
_____
_____
_____
_____
_____
_____

REVIEW

Real Numbers

Read each problem. Circle the letter of the best answer.

1 Which of the following is a rational number?

   A π **C**   5.77777…

   B $\sqrt{8}$ **D**   9.33444…

2 What type of decimal number is $7.0\overline{7}$?

   A   repeating   **C**   non-repeating

   B   terminating   **D**   non-terminating

3 Which of these numbers is **not** rational?

   A $3.0\overline{63}$ **C**   -1.45674

   B $\sqrt{49}$ **D**   5.123124…

4 Which of these numbers comes between $\sqrt{7}$ and $\frac{29}{7}$?

   A   2   **C** $\frac{\sqrt{14}}{2}$

   B   14   **D** $\sqrt{14}$

5 Which decimal **cannot** be written in fraction form?

   A $-0.\overline{987}$ **C**   2.35352…

   B   -0.457342   **D**   7.285285…

6 Which number is closest in value to X on the number line below?

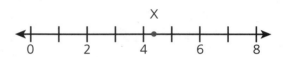

   A $\sqrt{14}$ **C** $\sqrt{24}$

   B $\sqrt{20}$ **D** $\sqrt{30}$

7 Which statement best describes the number –80.1801801…?

   A   It is rational because it is a repeating decimal.

   B   It is rational because it is a terminating decimal.

   C   It is irrational because it is a repeating decimal.

   D   It is irrational because it is a non-terminating decimal.

8 Which equation shows why $2.\overline{6}$ is a rational number?

   A $2.\overline{6} = 2.6$ **C** $2.\overline{6} = 2\frac{3}{5}$

   B $2.\overline{6} = 2\frac{2}{3}$ **D** $2.\overline{6} = 2.66$

Read each problem. Write your answer.

9 What two whole numbers does the value of $\sqrt{2} \cdot \pi$ lie between?

Answer ______________

10 Which of the numbers below are rational?

$\frac{41}{31}$ $\quad -\sqrt{\frac{9}{121}}$ $\quad$ 4.306009... $\quad \sqrt{24}$ $\quad$ -87.1939

Answer ______________

11 Which of these numbers has the greatest value?

$\sqrt{27}$ $\quad 2\pi$ $\quad \frac{51}{9}$ $\quad$ 6.124246...

Answer ______________

12 Show that -11.0027 is a rational number.

____

____

13 Write a rational number that lies between $\sqrt{2}$ and $\sqrt{3}$.

Answer ______________

14 Write a number between $\sqrt{\frac{1}{9}}$ and $\sqrt{\frac{1}{4}}$ that is irrational.

Answer ______________

15 Which is greater, π or $\frac{22}{7}$? Explain how you know.

____

____

____

16 Reilly changed $\frac{16}{11}$ to a decimal.

Part A Which type of decimal best describes $\frac{16}{11}$—terminating, not terminating, repeating, or not repeating? Explain how you know.

_____

_____

Part B Can a fraction be written as a non-terminating decimal? Explain how you know.

_____

_____

_____

_____

17 Dao writes the irrational number $\frac{\sqrt{10}}{2}$.

Part A Place a dot on the number line below to show the approximate location of $\frac{\sqrt{10}}{2}$.

Part B Explain how you found your answer.

_____

_____

_____

_____

Linear Relationships

- **Lesson 1 Proportional Relationships** reviews what proportional relationships are and compares them in equation and graphical forms.

- **Lesson 2 Graphing Linear Relationships** reviews how to graph linear equations through the origin on a coordinate plane and through any point on the *y*-axis of a coordinate plane.

- **Lesson 3 Solving Linear Equations** reviews how to solve linear equations with one solution, no solution, and infinitely many solutions.

- **Lesson 4 More Solving Equations** reviews how to solve multiple-step linear equations with rational number coefficients.

Proportional Relationships

8.EE.5, 8.EE.6

A **constant** is a value that does not change. In $y = 3x$, the constant is 3.

The **slope** of a line shows how the change in one variable relates to the change in the other variable.

$$\text{Slope} = \frac{\text{change in } y}{\text{change in } x}$$

For points (x_1, y_1) and (x_2, y_2), slope $= \frac{y_2 - y_1}{x_2 - x_1}$.

Slope is a constant since it is the same throughout a proportional relationship.

A **unit rate** is the ratio, or rate, for one unit of a given quantity.

The unit rate $\frac{\$3}{1 \text{ lb}}$ shows a cost of $3 per pound.

A **proportional relationship** exists between two quantities when one is a constant multiple of the other. In $y = mx$, a proportional relationship exists between the quantities x and y since the constant, m, multiplies x. In a proportional relationship, the constant is called the slope. Graphs and equations in the form $y = mx$ can be used to show proportional relationships.

Compare the equation $y = 2x$ with the proportional relationship graphed here.

Which has a greater slope, the equation or the line in the graph?

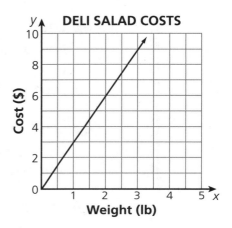

The slope of the equation $y = 2x$ is the constant, 2.

The slope of the line in the graph is the ratio that compares the change in cost to the change in weight.

- When the cost is $3, the weight is 1 lb: slope $= \frac{3}{1}$

- When the cost is $6, the weight is 2 lb: slope $= \frac{6}{2} = \frac{3}{1}$

- When the cost is $9, the weight is 3 lb: slope $= \frac{9}{3} = \frac{3}{1}$

The slope of the line is $\frac{3}{1}$ or 3.

Since $3 > 2$, the line in the graph has a greater slope.

In the graphed example above, you can see the slope is the same at each point. The slope simplifies to the same unit rate.

SAMPLE Similar triangles *GHJ* and *KHL* are shown on the coordinate plane.

Which statement must be true of the slope of $\overline{GH}$?

A It is the same as the slope of $\overline{GJ}$.

B It is the same as the slope of $\overline{KH}$.

C It is twice the slope of $\overline{GJ}$.

D It is twice the slope of $\overline{KH}$.

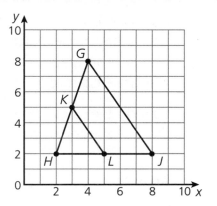

 The correct answer is B. Slope is the ratio of the change in *y*-values to the change in *x*-values. $\overline{GH}$ has endpoints (4, 8) and (2, 2). The slope of $\overline{GH}$ is $\frac{8-2}{4-2} = \frac{6}{2} = 3$. The slope of $\overline{GJ}$ is $\frac{8-2}{4-8} = \frac{6}{-4} = -\frac{3}{2}$. The slope of $\overline{KH}$ is $\frac{5-2}{3-2} = \frac{3}{1} = 3$. The slopes of $\overline{GH}$ and $\overline{KH}$ are both 3.

1 Lacey walks at a speed of 2.5 miles per hour. Which equation models this unit rate?

A $x = 2.5y$

B $x = 2.5 + y$

C $y = 2.5x$

D $y = 2.5 + x$

2 Triangle *MNP* is similar to triangle *QRS*.

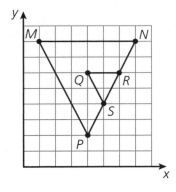

Which sides have the same slope?

A $\overline{MP}$ and $\overline{QS}$

B $\overline{MP}$ and $\overline{NP}$

C $\overline{QR}$ and $\overline{QS}$

D $\overline{QR}$ and $\overline{NP}$

3 The average speed, in miles per hour, a jet flies is graphed on the coordinate plane below.

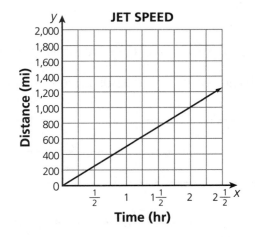

Which equation models this relationship?

A $y = 200x$

B $y = 500x$

C $y = 1,000x$

D $y = 2,000x$

SAMPLE The equation $y = 25x$ models the rate Tasha charges for tutoring x hours. This graph models the rate Lizzie charges for tutoring.

How do the rates Tasha and Lizzie charge for tutoring compare?

Answer _____

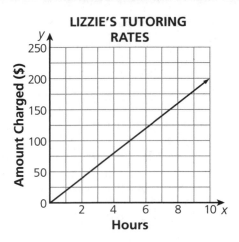

LIZZIE'S TUTORING RATES

The rate charged is the same as the slope of each model. The slope of the equation is 25, so Tasha charges $25 per hour. The slope of the line is y divided by x for any point on the graph, so the slope $= \frac{100}{5} = 20$. Lizzie charges $20 per hour of tutoring, which is $5 less per hour than Tasha.

4 Based on the graph above, write the equation that models Lizzie's charge for tutoring.

Answer _____

5 Triangles CDE and CFG are similar, as shown here.

Explain why the slope of $\overline{CE}$ is the same as the slope of $\overline{CG}$.

_____

_____

_____

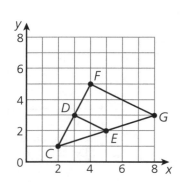

6 A factory makes 640 brushes in 4 hours. Does the equation $y = 150x$ model the number of brushes made each hour? Explain how you know.

_____

_____

UNIT 3 ▓▓
Linear Relationships

7 Gavin bought $2\frac{1}{2}$ cubic yards of topsoil for $75.

Part A What is the unit rate, in cost per cubic yard, for the topsoil?

What operation do you use to find the cost per yard?

Answer _____

Part B Write an equation in the form $y = mx$ to show this relationship. Explain how you know your equation is correct.

_____

_____

_____

8 Triangle *DEF* is shown here.

Triangle *DGH* is similar to triangle *DEF*.
The coordinates of vertex *H* are (10, 5)

Part A What are the coordinates of vertex *G?*

Answer _____

Part B Explain how you know.

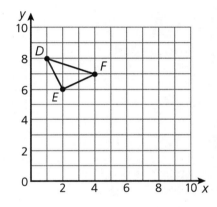

_____

_____

_____

Graphing Linear Relationships

8.EE.6

A coordinate plane has a horizontal axis, called the **x-axis,** and a vertical axis, called the **y-axis.**

To plot point (x, y) on a coordinate plane, first locate point x along the x-axis. From there, move y units up or down and plot the point.

The point (0, b) represents the y-intercept.

The slope of a line is the ratio of the change in the y-value over the change in the x-value. Slope is sometimes referred to as "rise over run."

Slope =

$$\frac{\text{change in } y}{\text{change in } x} = \frac{\text{rise}}{\text{run}}$$

For points (x_1, y_1) and (x_2, y_2), the slope formula is

$$\frac{y_2 - y_1}{x_2 - x_1}$$

To find the slope from a graph, you can count the rise and the run from any point on the line to the next point.

A graph of a linear relationship with the equation $y = mx$ goes through the **origin,** or center of a plane. The constant m represents the slope, or steepness, of the line.

Draw the graph of the equation $y = \frac{2}{3}x$ on a coordinate plane.

Make a table. Pick values for x. Find the values of y that make the equation true. Then plot the points and connect them.

x	$y = \frac{2}{3}x$
–3	–2
0	0
3	2
6	4

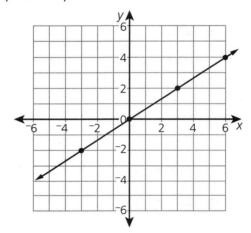

A linear relationship with the equation $y = mx + b$ goes through the point b on the y-axis. The point b is called the y-intercept.

Write the equation of the line shown on this coordinate plane.

The line touches the y-axis at –3. So the y-intercept is $b = -3$ or (0, –3). Use it and another point in the slope formula.

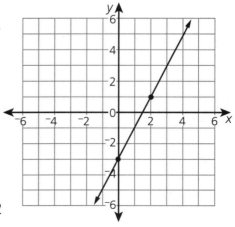

(0, –3) and (2, 1)

$$\text{slope} = m = \frac{1 - (-3)}{2 - 0} = \frac{4}{2} = 2$$

In $y = mx + b$, $m = 2$ and $b = -3$. So the equation of the line is $y = 2x - 3$.

SAMPLE What is the slope, *m,* and the
y-intercept, *b,* of this line?

A $m = 0$ and $b = -3$

B $m = -3$ and $b = 0$

C $m = 0$ and $b = -\frac{1}{3}$

D $m = -\frac{1}{3}$ and $b = 0$

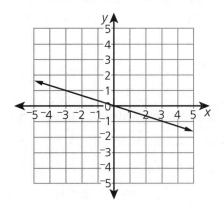

  The correct answer is D. The *y*-intercept, *b,* is the point where the line touches the *y*-axis. Since the line goes through the origin, the *y*-intercept is 0. From the origin, count the rise over the run to the next point of the graph. This is the slope. From the origin, "rise" 1 unit up and "run" 3 units left to the next point: $m = \frac{\text{rise}}{\text{run}} = \frac{+1}{-3} = -\frac{1}{3}$.

1 Which equation has a slope of −6 and a *y*-intercept of 5?

A $y = 5x - 6$ **C** $y = -(5x + 6)$

B $y = -6x + 5$ **D** $y = -(6x + 5)$

2 Which statement is true of *m,* the slope of this line?

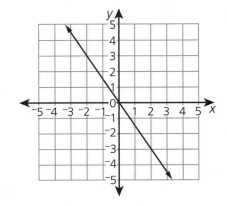

A $m < -1$ **C** $0 < m < 1$

B $-1 < m < 0$ **D** $m > 1$

3 Tony graphed the line $y = \frac{5}{2}x + 2$ on this coordinate plane.

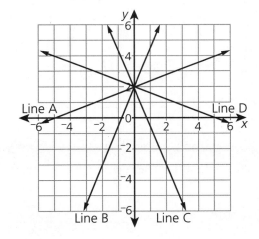

Which line did Tony graph?

A line A   **C** line C

B line B   **D** line D

SAMPLE What is the slope of this line?

Answer _____

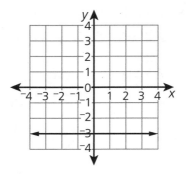

Locate two points on the line. Then use the slope formula: slope $= \dfrac{y_2 - y_1}{x_2 - x_1}$.

For points (0, –3) and (2, –3), slope $= \dfrac{-3 - (-3)}{2 - 0} = \dfrac{0}{2}$. The slope is 0.

4 What is the equation of the line shown on this coordinate plane?

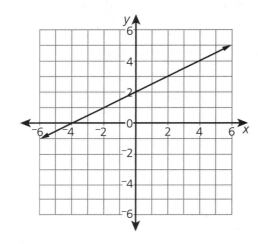

Answer _____

5 Hakim graphs a line that slants downward from left to right. What must be true of the slope of this line?

Answer _____

6 Paige graphs the equation $y = -5x + 4$. What are the slope and the y-intercept of this equation?

Slope _____ y-intercept _____

7 Eric wants to graph the line $y = -x - 4$.

Part A Make a table of values to find five points on the graph of this line.

Be careful when subtracting numbers with negative signs.

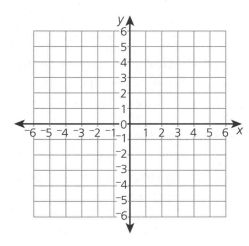

x	y

Part B Graph this line on the coordinate plane above.

8 Willow has the equations $y = 2x$ and $y = 2x + 3$.

Part A Graph and label the equations on the coordinate plane below.

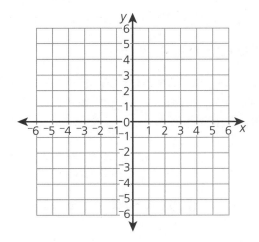

Part B How are these lines alike? How are they different? Explain.

_____

_____

_____

Solving Linear Equations

8.EE.7.a

Addition and subtraction are inverse operations. Multiplication and division are inverse operations.

To keep an equation balanced, always perform the same operation to both sides.

$$n - 3 = 8$$
$$n - 3 + 3 = 8 + 3$$

$$\frac{p}{2} = 5$$

$$\frac{p}{2} \cdot 2 = 5 \cdot 2$$

You can check that an answer is correct by substituting the value of the variable back into the original equation. It should make the equation true.

$$3x - 5 = 7 \quad \text{for } x = 4$$
$$3(4) - 5 = 7$$
$$12 - 5 = 7$$
$$7 = 7 \quad \text{true}$$

An **equation** is a number sentence that shows two expressions are equal. An equation can contain numbers and variables. A **variable** is a symbol or letter that represents an unknown number.

A **solution** to an equation is the value of the variable that makes the equation true. To solve an equation for a variable, use inverse operations. **Inverse operations** are like opposite operations. They "undo" each other.

Solve the equation $-9x = 3$.

In this equation, -9 multiplies x. Divide both side of the equation by -9 to undo the multiplication and solve for x.

$$-9x \div (-9) = 3 \div (-9)$$
$$x = -\frac{1}{3}$$

Some equations require two steps to solve. For these, first undo the addition or subtraction. Then undo the multiplication or division.

Solve the equation $4x + 9 = 5$.

The two operations in this equation are multiplication and addition. First, subtract 9 from both sides of the equation to undo the addition.

$$4x + 9 - 9 = 5 - 9$$
$$4x = -4$$

Next, divide both sides by 4 to undo the multiplication.

$$4x \div 4 = -4 \div 4$$
$$x = -1$$

Check: $4(-1) + 9 = 5$
$$-4 + 9 = 5$$
$$5 = 5$$

Since $5 = 5$ is a true statement, $x = -1$ is the solution.

UNIT 3 ▓▓
Linear Relationships

SAMPLE What is the solution to $-12 = 3x - 3$?

    A -5   **B** -3   **C** 3   **D** 5

> The correct answer is B. This equation uses multiplication and subtraction. First add 3 to both sides to undo the subtraction: $-12 + 3 = 3x - 3 + 3$, so $-9 = 3x$. Then divide both sides by 3 to undo the multiplication: $-9 ÷ 3 = 3x ÷ 3$, so $-3 = x$.

1 What is the first operation you should use to solve the equation $5x + 4 = 1$?

  A addition   **C** multiplication

  B subtraction   **D** division

2 What is the solution to the equation $d - 14 = -6$?

  A $d = -20$ **C** $d = 8$

  B $d = -8$ **D** $d = 20$

3 Which steps should be taken to solve the equation $\frac{y}{6} - 2 = 5$?

  A first add, then multiply

  B first multiply, then add

  C first divide, then subtract

  D first subtract, then divide

4 What is the solution to the equation $8r + 6 = 2$?

  A $r = 1$ **C** $r = -1$

  B $r = \frac{1}{2}$ **D** $r = -\frac{1}{2}$

5 What value of z makes this equation true?

$$-2z + 5 = -11$$

  A $z = 8$ **C** $z = -3$

  B $z = 3$ **D** $z = -8$

6 What is the solution to this equation?

$$\frac{m}{4} + 3 = -1$$

  A $m = -1$ **C** $m = -8$

  B $m = -7$ **D** $m = -16$

7 What value of q makes the equation true?

$$3q + 11 = 4$$

  A 5   **C** $-\frac{7}{3}$

  B 3   **D** $-9\frac{2}{3}$

8 What value of k makes this equation true?

$$7 - \frac{k}{2} = 1$$

  A -12   **C** 10

  B -10   **D** 12

SAMPLE Madison thinks the solution to the equation $2z - 17 = 11$ is –3. Is she correct? Explain.

Answer _____

  No, Madison is not correct. To check if –3 is a solution, substitute that number for z into the equation: $2(-3) - 17 = 11$. Then simplify and see if the result is true: $-6 - 17 = 11 \rightarrow -23 = 11$. Since $-23 \neq 11$, the number –3 is not the solution.

9 What value of n makes the equation $\frac{n}{3} - 2 = 4$ true? Show your work.

Answer _____

10 Write a two-step equation that has –5 as its solution.

Answer _____

11 Is –7 the solution to the equation $\frac{w}{7} + 2 = -1$? Explain how you know.

_____

_____

_____

12 Ivan wants to solve the equation $-6h + 4 = 8$.

Part A What value of h makes this equation true? Show your work.

Answer _____

Part B Show how to check your answer.

13 Juliana wrote the equation $-\dfrac{x}{3} - 8 = 4$.

Part A What steps should be used to solve this equation?

_____

_____

_____

_____

_____

What operation should be "undone" first? What inverse operation should be used to do this?

Part B What is the solution to the equation? Explain how you found your answer.

_____

_____

_____

More Solving Equations

8.EE.7.a, b

A **term** is a part of an expression or equation that is separated by addition or subtraction.

$$3x + 6xy - 30$$

Terms are $3x$, $6xy$, and -30.

Like terms are terms that have the same variable parts. Numbers without variables are also like terms.

The **distributive property** states that the product of a number and the sum of two numbers is the same as the sum of the products of the number and each part of the sum.

$$a(b + c) = ab + ac$$
$$6(x + 2) = 6x + 12$$

For any solution to an equation where x represents a variable and a and b represent numbers, if

- $x = a$, the equation has one solution.
- $a = b$, the equation has no solution.
- $a = a$, the equation has an infinite, or unlimited, number of solutions.

You used inverse operations to solve linear equations involving one or two steps. For equations involving more than two steps, like terms need to be combined before inverse operations are used.

Solve the equation $4(m - 2) = 3m + 5$.

First, use the distributive property to simplify the equation.

$$4(m - 2) = 3m + 5$$
$$4m - 8 = 3m + 5$$

Next, bring all variable terms to one side of the equation. Do this by subtracting $3m$ from both sides.

$$4m - 8 - 3m = 3m + 5 - 3m$$
$$m - 8 = 5$$

Then, use inverse operations to solve.

$$m - 8 + 8 = 5 + 8$$
$$m = 13$$

Some equations, like the one above, have exactly one solution. Other equations have no solution or many solutions that make the equation true.

How many solutions does this equation have?

$$4p + 2 = 5p - 3 - p$$

First, combine like terms on the right side of the equation.

$$4p + 2 = 5p - 3 - p$$
$$4p + 2 = 4p - 3$$

Next, bring all variable terms to one side of the equation.

$$4p + 2 - 4p = 4p - 3 - 4p$$
$$2 = -3 \qquad \leftarrow \text{not true}$$

Since $2 \neq -3$, this equation has no solution.

Read each problem. Circle the letter of the best answer.

SAMPLE How many solutions does this equation have?

$$\frac{5}{3}y - \frac{5}{3}(y + 3) = -5$$

A 0   **B** exactly 1   **C** 2   **D** more than 2

The correct answer is D. Solve the equation for y. Start by distributing $-\frac{5}{3}$: $\frac{5}{3}y - \frac{5}{3}y - 5 = -5$. Then combine the variable terms: $0 - 5 = -5$, or $-5 = -5$. Since -5 always equals itself, this means the equation has infinitely many solutions.

1 What are the like terms in this expression?

$$5m - 5 + 5n + 1$$

A $5m$ and -5 **C** $5m$ and $5n$

B -5 and 1 **D** $5m$, -5, and $5n$

2 What is the solution to this equation?

$$2 - 3n + 4n = 3n + 6$$

A $n = 2$ **C** $n = -1$

B $n = 1$ **D** $n = -2$

3 What is the solution to this equation?

$$-0.5z + 1.25 = 3.5z + 0.75$$

A $z = 0.125$ **C** $z = 0.5$

B $z = 0.167$ **D** $z = 0.75$

4 Which equation has no solution?

A $3x - 4 = 4x - 3$

B $x + 5 + 2x = 2x + 5$

C $2(x + 2) - x = x + 2$

D $6x + 1 - 6 = -5x + 6$

5 What value of q makes this equation true?

$$4q + 5 - q = 2(q - 3)$$

A -11 **C** 2

B -2 **D** 11

6 How many solutions does this equation have?

$$9w + 1 = 9(w + 1)$$

A 0 **C** 2

B exactly 1   **D** more than 2

7 What is the solution to this equation?

$$\frac{3}{4}(p + 12) = \frac{1}{2}(p - 6)$$

A $p = 72$ **C** $p = -12$

B $p = 24$ **D** $p = -48$

8 What value of y makes this equation true?

$$12y - 3(y - 3) = 6y + 8 - (y + 2)$$

A -1.25 **C** 3.25

B -0.75 **D** 3.75

SAMPLE Donovan solved the equation $3(x + 1) = 3x + 3$. He thinks there is no solution to the equation since there are no variables in the equation after they are combined. Is Donovan correct? Explain how you know.

Answer _____

No, Donovan is not correct. Solve this equation for x: $3x + 3 = 3x + 3$. Combine the variables: $3x + 3 - 3x = 3x + 3 - 3x$. This leaves $3 = 3$. Since this is always true, this means there are infinitely many solutions for x that make this equation true.

9 What value of x makes the equation $2(x - 1) = -x + 5$ true? Show your work.

Answer _____

10 How many solutions are there to the equation below?

$$b + \frac{1}{4} - b = 2b + \frac{1}{4}$$

Answer _____

11 Explain how to tell if an equation has no solution.

_____

_____

_____

_____

12 Garrett wrote the equation $5(k - 3) = 3(k - 5)$.

Part A What value of k makes this equation true?

Answer _____

Part B Explain how you know.

_____

_____

_____

13 Tamara solved the equation below.

$$6x + 2(x + 3) = 3x + 5x + 6$$

She got $x = 3$ for a solution.

Part A Is Tamara's solution correct? Show why or why not.

Answer _____

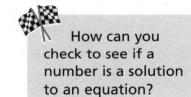

How can you check to see if a number is a solution to an equation?

Part B Are there any other solutions to this equation? Explain how you know.

_____

_____

_____

REVIEW

Linear Relationships

Read each problem. Circle the letter of the best answer.

1 Which equation has a slope of $\frac{3}{2}$ and a y-intercept of $-\frac{1}{2}$?

A $y = -\frac{1}{2}x + \frac{3}{2}$ **C** $y = -\left(\frac{1}{2}x + \frac{3}{2}\right)$

B $y = \frac{3}{2}x - \frac{1}{2}$ **D** $y = -\left(\frac{3}{2}x - \frac{1}{2}\right)$

2 What value of k makes the equation true?

$$2k + 19 = 5$$

A –12   **C** 7

B –7   **D** 12

3 Which equation models this relationship?

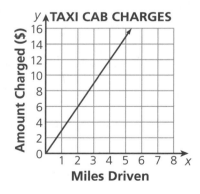

A $y = \frac{1}{2}x$ **C** $y = \frac{1}{3}x$

B $y = 2x$ **D** $y = 3x$

4 Which steps should be taken to solve the equation $-5n - 3 = 8$?

A first add, then divide

B first divide, then add

C first subtract, then multiply

D first multiply, then subtract

5 Similar triangles *LMN* and *PQN* are shown on this coordinate plane.

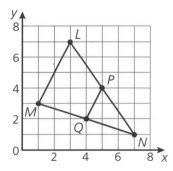

Which statement must be true of the slope of $\overline{PN}$?

A It is half the slope of $\overline{LN}$.

B It is half the slope of $\overline{QN}$.

C It is the same as the slope of $\overline{LN}$.

D It is the same as the slope of $\overline{QN}$.

6 What is the solution to this equation?

$$6(p + 0.4) = 5(p - 1.2)$$

Answer _____

7 What value of y makes the equation $\frac{y}{8} + 1 = -5$ true?

Answer _____

8 How many solutions are there to the equation below— 0, exactly 1, or more than 1?

$$3(v - 5) + 3 = 4(v - 3) - v$$

Answer _____

9 Is 4 the solution to the equation $-2n + 5 = -3$? Explain how you know.

_____

_____

10 The equation $y = 20x$ models the average number of pages Ewan reads in x hours. This graph models the average number of pages Phil reads in x hours.

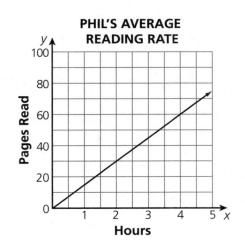

PHIL'S AVERAGE READING RATE

How do the average reading rates for Ewan and Phil compare?

_____

_____

11 Karina graphed the line on this coordinate plane.

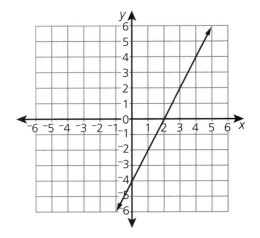

Part A What is the *y*-intercept of this line?

Answer _____

Part B Write an equation in the form $y = mx + b$ that models this line. Explain how you know your answer is correct.

_____

_____

_____

12 Lucas wrote the equation $7m - 2(m + 3) = m + 6 + 4m$.

Part A What value of *m* makes this equation true?

Answer _____

Part B Explain how you know.

_____

_____

_____

_____

UNIT 3 ✠✠
Linear Relationships

UNIT
4

Systems of Linear Equations

● **Lesson 1 Solving Systems of Equations Graphically** reviews what systems of linear equations are and shows how to solve them graphically.

● **Lesson 2 Solving Systems of Equations by Elimination** reviews how to use the elimination method to solve systems of linear equations.

● **Lesson 3 Solving Systems of Equations by Substitution** reviews how to use the substitution method to solve systems of linear equations.

● **Lesson 4 Problem Solving with Systems of Equations** reviews how to write and solve systems of linear equations to solve real-world and mathematical problems.

Solving Systems of Equations Graphically

8.EE.8.a, b

It helps to have equations written in slope-intercept form when graphing them.

The **slope-intercept form** of an equation is
$y = mx + b$,
where m is the slope and b is the y-intercept.

To rewrite an equation in slope-intercept form, solve it for y.

$$2x + y = 7$$
$$2x - 2x + y = -2x + 7$$
$$y = -2x + 7$$

One solution

No solution

Infinitely many solutions

An **infinite** number of solutions means there are an uncountable number of solutions.

A **system of linear equations** is a set of two or more linear equations. The solution to a system of linear equations is the point or points that are common to both equations in the set. To find the solution to a system of equations, you can graph the lines on a coordinate plane and identify where they intersect.

Graph the system $\begin{cases} y = 2x - 3 \\ x + 2y = 4 \end{cases}$ to find its solution.

The first equation is in slope-intercept form. Rewrite the second equation so it is also in slope-intercept form.

$$x + 2y = 4 \quad \rightarrow \quad 2y = -x + 4 \quad \rightarrow \quad y = -\frac{1}{2} + 2$$

Graph the system $\begin{cases} y = 2x - 3 \\ y = -\frac{1}{2}x + 2 \end{cases}$ on a coordinate plane.

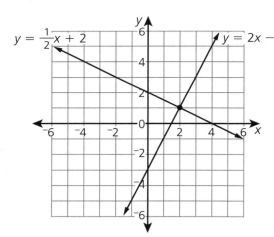

The solution is the point (2, 1) since this is where the lines intersect.

A system of equations has exactly

- *one solution* when each equation in the system has a different slope,

- *no solution* when each equation in the system has the same slope but different y-intercepts, and

- *infinitely many solutions* if each equation in the system has the same slope and the same y-intercept.

SAMPLE Which statement best describes the solution to $\begin{cases} y = x + 4 \\ x - y = 4 \end{cases}$?

    A   The solution is (0, 4).   **C**   There is no solution.

    B   The solution is (−4, 0).   **D**   There are infinitely many solutions.

> The correct answer is C. Rewrite the system so that both equations are in slope-intercept form: $\begin{cases} y = x + 4 \\ y = x - 4 \end{cases}$. Both equations have the same slope, 1, but different y-intercepts. The lines will be parallel and never intersect. So, the system has no solution.

1 What is the solution to the system of equations shown on this graph?

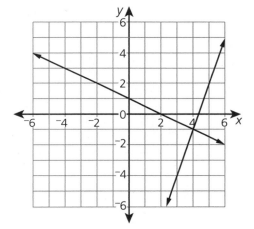

    A   (1, 4)   **C**   (4, 1)

    B   (−1, 4)   **D**   (4, −1)

2 How many solutions does this system of linear equations have?

$$\begin{cases} x + 3y = 1 \\ 2x + 6y = 2 \end{cases}$$

    A   0   **C**   exactly 2

    B   exactly 1   **D**   infinitely many

3 Which pair of lines represents a system of equations with the solution (−1, −3)?

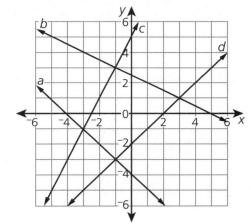

    A a and c **C** b and d

    B b and c **D** d and a

4 Francine wants to graph the system of equations $\begin{cases} 3x - y = 4 \\ 2x + 3y = -6 \end{cases}$. Which shows how she should rewrite these equations before graphing?

    A $\begin{cases} y = 3x + 4 \\ y = -\frac{2}{3}x - 2 \end{cases}$ **C** $\begin{cases} y = 3x - 4 \\ y = -\frac{2}{3}x - 2 \end{cases}$

    B $\begin{cases} y = 3x - 4 \\ y = -\frac{3}{2}x - 3 \end{cases}$ **D** $\begin{cases} y = 3x + 4 \\ y = -\frac{3}{2}x - 3 \end{cases}$

SAMPLE Is the point (−3, 5) a solution to this system of equations? Explain how you know.

$$\begin{cases} 3x + 2y = 1 \\ 2x - y = -1 \end{cases}$$

Answer _____

   The point (−3, 5) means that $x = -3$ and $y = 5$. Substitute these values into each equation. If both equations are true, then this point is a solution to the system. The equation $3(-3) + 2(5) = 1$ simplifies to $-9 + 10 = 1$, or $1 = 1$. This is true. The equation $2(-3) - 5 = -1$ simplifies to $-6 - 5 = -1$, or $-11 = -1$. This is not true. Since the point (−3, 5) does not make both equations in the system true, it is not a solution.

5 Graph and label this system of equations on the coordinate plane. Then identify the solution.

$$\begin{cases} y = -x + 5 \\ y = \frac{3}{2}x \end{cases}$$

Answer _____

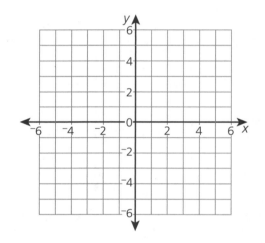

6 Nerina graphed the equations $2x + 3y = 2$ and $y = \frac{2}{3}x - 2$ on this coordinate plane.

Nerina thinks the solution to this system of equations is (3, 0). Is she correct? Explain how you know.

_____

_____

_____

_____

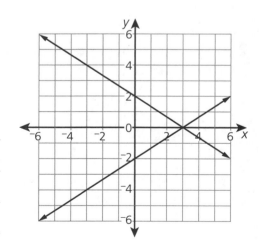

UNIT 4 ▪▪
Systems of Linear Equations

7 Look at this system of equations.

$$\begin{cases} y = -\frac{5}{2}x + 1 \\ 5x + 2y = -6 \end{cases}$$

Part A Graph and label this system of equations on the coordinate plane.

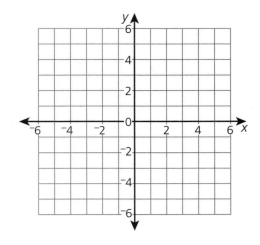

Part B What is solution to this system of equations? Explain how you know.

Compare the slopes and the *y*-intercepts of the equations. What do they tell you about the solution?

_____

_____

_____

_____

Solving Systems of Equations by Elimination

8.EE.8.b

It doesn't matter which variable, *x* or *y*, you choose to eliminate. You should still be able to find the full solution.

The **additive inverse property** says if you add a value and its opposite, the answer is always 0.

$$a + (-a) = 0$$
$$3 + (-3) = 0$$
$$5x + (-5x) = 0$$

When multiplying an equation by a factor, be sure to multiply *all* terms of the equation by the factor. This will keep it balanced.

Remember that some systems of equations can have no solution or infinitely many solutions.

For systems with no solution, the sum of the equations would be $0 = a$, where $a \neq 0$, which is false.

For systems with infinitely many solutions, the sum of the equations would be $0 = 0$, which is always true.

Systems of equations can be solved using algebra. One way is the elimination method. Using **elimination,** the equations are added together to eliminate, or remove, one of the variable terms.

What is the solution to $\begin{cases} 2x + y = 9 \\ 3x - 2y = -4 \end{cases}$?

To eliminate a variable term, additive inverses need to be combined. If each term in the first equation is multiplied by 2, $2y$ will result in the first equation. This can then be added to $-2y$ in the second equation to eliminate the *y* term.

$$2(2x + y = 9) \quad \rightarrow \quad \begin{array}{r} 4x + 2y = 18 \\ +3x - 2y = -4 \\ \hline 7x + 0 = 14, \text{ so } x = 2 \end{array}$$

Substitute $x = 2$ into either equation in the system. Solve for *y*.

$$2(2) + y = 9$$
$$4 + y = 9, \text{ so } y = 5$$

(2, 5) is the solution to this system of equations.

Sometimes both equations in a system need to be multiplied by a factor to form terms that can be eliminated.

What is the solution to $\begin{cases} 2x - 3y = 7 \\ 3x + 4y = 2 \end{cases}$?

Multiply the first equation by 4. Multiply the second equation by 3. Then add. This will eliminate the *y* term.

$$\begin{array}{r} 4(2x - 3y = 7) \quad \rightarrow \quad 8x - 12y = 28 \\ 3(3x + 4y = 2) \quad \rightarrow \quad +9x + 12y = 6 \\ \hline 17x + 0 = 34, \text{ so } x = 2 \end{array}$$

Substitute $x = 2$ into either equation. Then solve for *y*.

$$2(2) - 3y = 7$$
$$4 - 3y = 7$$
$$-3y = 3, \text{ so } y = -1$$

(2, -1) is the solution.

SAMPLE Which best describes the solution to $\begin{cases} -4x + 6y = -2 \\ 2x - 3y = 1 \end{cases}$?

A (0, 0)

B (-2, 1)

C no solution

D infinitely many solutions

> The correct answer is D. Multiply the second equation by 2 to get terms that are additive inverses: $2(2x - 3y = 1)$ is $4x - 6y = 2$. Add the equations:
> $$-4x + 6y = -2$$
> $$\underline{+4x - 6y = 2}$$
> $$0 + 0 = 0$$
> Since $0 = 0$ is always true, there are infinitely many solutions for this system of equations.

1 Look at this system of equations.

$$\begin{cases} 5x + 2y = -1 \\ x + 3y = -8 \end{cases}$$

Which of the following statements describes a possible first step in solving this system using elimination?

A Multiply the first equation by -1.

B Multiply the second equation by -1.

C Multiply the first equation by -5.

D Multiply the second equation by -5.

2 What is the solution to this system of equations?

$$\begin{cases} x + y = 4 \\ x - y = -2 \end{cases}$$

A (1, 3)

B (2, 2)

C (3, 1)

D (4, -2)

3 Marcus wants to add the equations to eliminate one of the variable terms in this system of equations.

$$\begin{cases} 3x + 2y = -5 \\ 2x + 5y = -7 \end{cases}$$

Which of the following shows the correct factors needed to eliminate a variable term when adding the equations?

A $\begin{cases} 2(3x + 2y = -5) \\ 3(2x + 5y = -7) \end{cases}$

B $\begin{cases} -2(3x + 2y = -5) \\ 3(2x + 5y = -7) \end{cases}$

C $\begin{cases} 3(3x + 2y = -5) \\ 3(2x + 5y = -7) \end{cases}$

D $\begin{cases} 3(3x + 2y = -5) \\ -3(2x + 5y = -7) \end{cases}$

4 What is the solution to $\begin{cases} 6x - 5y = 28 \\ 4x - 3y = 18 \end{cases}$?

A (2, -2)

B (2, -3)

C (3, -2)

D (3, -3)

SAMPLE Jazmin and Monelle solve this system of equations using the elimination method.

$$\begin{cases} 5x - y = -2 \\ x + 2y = -1 \end{cases}$$

Jazmin multiplies the first equation by 2 and then adds the equations. Monelle multiplies the second equation by –5 and then adds the equations. Which person uses the elimination method correctly?

Answer _____

They both use the elimination method correctly. By multiplying the first equation by 2, Jazmin can eliminate the y term and then solve for x. By multiplying the second equation by –5, Monelle can eliminate the x term and then solve for y. Both ways will lead to the full solution for this system of equations.

5 What is the solution to this system of equations? Show your work.

$$\begin{cases} x + 2y = 8 \\ 3x + 4y = 20 \end{cases}$$

Answer _____

6 How many solutions are there to this system of equations?

$$\begin{cases} -2x - y = 12 \\ 4x + 2y = -12 \end{cases}$$

Answer _____

Read each problem. Write your answer to each part.

7 Look at this system of equations.

$$\begin{cases} 2x = y + 7 \\ x + 2y = 6 \end{cases}$$

Part A What is the solution to this system of equations?

Answer ____________

Part B Explain how you found your answer.

____

____

____

____

8 There are infinitely many solutions to this system of equations.

$$\begin{cases} -x + 3y = 8 \\ x + py = q \end{cases}$$

Part A What must be the values of p and q?

Answer ______________________

Part B Explain how you know.

____

____

____

____

What result would you get by adding equations that have infinitely many solutions?

It doesn't matter which equation or which variable, x or y, you choose to solve for. You should still be able to find the solution.

It is easier to solve for a variable that has 1 as a coefficient.

$$1x = x$$

Remember to fully distribute the factor into each term within the parentheses.

$$4(2x + 7) = 4(2x) + 4(7)$$
$$= 8x + 28$$

Remember that some systems of equations can have no solution or infinitely many solutions.

For systems with no solution, the substituted equation would result in $a = b$, which is false.

For systems with infinitely many solutions, the substituted equation would result in $a = a$, which is always true.

Another way to solve systems of equations algebraically is the substitution method. In **substitution,** one equation is written in terms of a single variable. Then the expression equal to that variable is substituted into the other equation.

What is the solution to this system of equations?

$$\begin{cases} x - 3y = 2 \\ 2x - 5y = 2 \end{cases}$$

Set the first equation equal to x.

$$x - 3y = 2 \quad \rightarrow \quad x = 3y + 2$$

Substitute $3y + 2$ for x in the second equation.

$$2(3y + 2) - 5y = 2$$

Solve the equation for y.

$$2(3y + 2) - 5y = 2 \quad \rightarrow \quad 6y + 4 - 5y = 2$$
$$y + 4 = 2$$
$$y = -2$$

Substitute $y = -2$ into either equation in the system. Solve for x.

$$x - 3(-2) = 2$$
$$x + 6 = 2$$
$$x = -4$$

Check that $x = -4$ and $y = -2$, or $(-4, -2)$ is the solution. Substitute both values into each equation. See if the equations are both true.

$$x - 3y = 2 \qquad\qquad 2x - 5y = 2$$
$$-4 - 3(-2) = 2 \qquad\qquad 2(-4) - 5(-2) = 2$$
$$-4 + 6 = 2 \qquad\qquad -8 + 10 = 2$$
$$2 = 2 \quad \text{true} \qquad\qquad 2 = 2 \quad \text{true}$$

Both equations are true, so $(-4, -2)$ is the solution.

SAMPLE Which best describes the solution to $\begin{cases} 6x + 3y = 4 \\ 2x + y = 2 \end{cases}$?

- **A** (0, 0)
- **C** no solution
- **B** (4, 2)
- **D** infinitely many solutions

The correct answer is C. Solve the second equation for y: $y = -2x + 2$. Substitute the expression $-2x + 2$ for y in the first equation: $6x + 3(-2x + 2) = 4$. Then solve for x: $6x - 6x + 6 = 4$, $6 = 4$. Since this is false, there are no solutions to this system of equations.

1 Is (-5, 3) a solution to this system of equations?

$$\begin{cases} x + y = -2 \\ -2x + y = 13 \end{cases}$$

- **A** Yes, because it is a solution to both equations.
- **B** No, because it is not a solution to the first equation.
- **C** No, because it is not a solution to the second equation.
- **D** No, because it is not a solution to either equation.

2 Look at this system of equations.

$$\begin{cases} x + 4y = 3 \\ y = -1 \end{cases}$$

What is the solution to this system?

- **A** (-1, -1)
- **C** (1, -1)
- **B** (-1, 7)
- **D** (7, -1)

3 What is the solution to this system of equations?

$$\begin{cases} x = 2y - 1 \\ x = y + 3 \end{cases}$$

- **A** (2, 5)
- **C** (5, 2)
- **B** (4, 7)
- **D** (7, 4)

4 What is the solution to this system of equations?

$$\begin{cases} 2x = -6y + 4 \\ 3x + 9y = 6 \end{cases}$$

- **A** (0, 0)
- **B** (2, 0)
- **C** no solution
- **D** infinitely many solutions

5 What is the solution to this system of equations?

$$\begin{cases} x = -3y - 2 \\ y = x + 2 \end{cases}$$

- **A** (2, 0)
- **C** (0, 2)
- **B** (-2, 0)
- **D** (0, -2)

SAMPLE What is the solution to this system of equations?

$$\begin{cases} y = \frac{1}{2}x + 4 \\ y = -x + 1 \end{cases}$$

Answer _____

 Since both equations are solved for y, set the expressions $\frac{1}{2}x + 4$ and $-x + 1$ equal to each: $\frac{1}{2}x + 4 = -x + 1$. Then solve for x: $\frac{3}{2}x + 4 = 1$, $\frac{3}{2}x = -3$, so $x = -2$. Substitute $x = -2$ into either equation and solve for y: $y = -(-2) + 1 = 3$. The solution is $(-2, 3)$.

6 How many solutions are there to this system of equations?

$$\begin{cases} x + y = 5 \\ x = y + 5 \end{cases}$$

Answer _____

7 What is the solution to this system of equations? Show your work.

$$\begin{cases} -x - 2y = -3 \\ 3x + 3y = 0 \end{cases}$$

Answer _____

8 Look at this system of equations.

$$\begin{cases} x + y = -2 \\ 2x + y = 3 \end{cases}$$

Part A What is the solution to this system of equations?

      Answer _____

Part B Explain how you found your answer.

_____

_____

_____

_____

9 Lamont wrote this system of equations.

$$\begin{cases} x = 2y + 2 \\ y = x + 1 \end{cases}$$

Part A Lamont started to solve this system of equations using the equation $2y + 2 = x + 1$. Will this equation help him get the solution to this system of equations? Explain how you know.

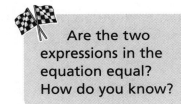

Are the two expressions in the equation equal? How do you know?

_____

_____

_____

Part B What is the solution? Show your work.

      Answer _____

Problem Solving with Systems of Equations

8.EE.8.c

The formula for the perimeter of a rectangle with length *l* and width *w* is $P = 2l + 2w$.

Use the elimination method to solve a system of equations if a variable term can easily be canceled by adding the equations.

Use the substitution method if at least one of the equations can easily be solved for either variable.

You can check your solution by substituting the values for *x* and *y* into both equations in the system. Each equation should result in true statements.

Some real-life problems can be solved using a system of equations. To do this, translate the problem situation into an algebra sentence involving two variables. Then solve the system using one of the methods you previously learned.

The length of a rectangle is three inches shorter than twice its width. The perimeter of the rectangle is 30 inches. What are the length and the width of this rectangle?

Write equations to represent the given information. Let *l* = length and *w* = width.

"length is three inches shorter than twice its width" translates to $l = 2w - 3$.

"perimeter of the rectangle is 30 inches" translates to $2l + 2w = 30$.

The system of equations is $\begin{cases} l = 2w - 3 \\ 2l + 2w = 30 \end{cases}$.

Choose a method to solve the system of equations. Since one equation is solved for *l*, the substitution method is good to use.

Solve the system of equations. Substitute $2w - 3$ for *l* into the second equation and solve for *w*.

$$2(2w - 3) + 2w = 30$$
$$4w - 6 + 2w = 30$$
$$6w - 6 = 30$$
$$6w = 36$$
$$w = 6$$

Use *w* to solve for *l*:
$$l = 2(6) - 3$$
$$l = 12 - 3$$
$$l = 9$$

The length is 9 inches and the width is 6 inches.

SAMPLE Carter has a total of 15 dimes and quarters. The total value of these coins is $2.85. How many dimes and how many quarters does Carter have?

   A   5 dimes and 10 quarters   **C**   9 dimes and 6 quarters

   B   6 dimes and 9 quarters   **D**   10 dimes and 5 quarters

The correct answer is B. Write a system of equations to find the numbers of dimes, d, and of quarters, q: $\begin{cases} d + q = 15 \\ 0.10d + 0.25q = 2.85 \end{cases}$. Solve this system using the substitution method. Rewrite the first equation to equal d: $d = -q + 15$. Substitute $-q + 15$ for d in the second equation: $0.10(-q + 15) + 0.25q = 2.85$. Solve for q: $-0.10q + 1.5 + 0.25q = 2.85$, $0.15q = 1.35$, so $q = 9$. Use that value to find d: $d + 9 = 15$, so $d = 6$. Carter has 6 dimes and 9 quarters.

1 A quiz has 26 questions and is worth 100 points. Some questions are worth 2 points. The rest are worth 5 points. Which system of equations can be used to find the number of each type of question?

  A $\begin{cases} x + y = 26 \\ 2x + 5y = 100 \end{cases}$ **C** $\begin{cases} x + 2y = 26 \\ x + 5y = 100 \end{cases}$

  B $\begin{cases} x + y = 100 \\ 2x + 5y = 26 \end{cases}$ **D** $\begin{cases} 2x + 2y = 26 \\ 5x + 5y = 100 \end{cases}$

2 A company sells plastic and metal fittings. A shipment of 200 plastic and 50 metal fittings costs $650. A shipment of 100 plastic and 150 metal fittings costs $950. What is the total cost of one plastic and one metal fitting?

  A $5   **C** $10

  B $7   **D** $15

3 Zoey and Rachel had some crackers and nuts for a snack. Zoey ate 4 crackers and 20 nuts. This totaled 240 calories. Rachel ate 10 crackers and 10 nuts. This totaled 280 calories. Which statement is true?

  A   Each nut has 16 calories.

  B   Each nut has 20 calories.

  C   Each cracker has 16 calories.

  D   Each cracker has 20 calories.

4 Leah wants to join a health club. One club charges a $120 registration fee and $30 a month to be a member. Another club charges no registration fee and $45 a month to be a member. After how many months is the cost of these two health clubs the same?

  A 3   **C** 8

  B 6   **D** 12

SAMPLE Zack invested money in a savings account that earns 3% interest in one year. He invested $200 more than this in another savings account that earns 5% interest each year. After one year, Zack earned $58 in interest. How much money did he invest in each savings account?

Answer _____

Let x = the amount invested at 3% and y = the amount invested at 5%. The system of equations for this is $\begin{cases} y = x + 200 \\ 0.03x + 0.05y = 58 \end{cases}$.

Use the substitution method to solve for x and y:
$0.03x + 0.05(x + 200) = 58$, $0.03x + 0.05x + 10 = 58$,
$0.08x = 48$, so $x = \$600$ at 3% interest. Use the value of x to find y:
$y = 600 + 200 = \$800$ at 5% interest.

5 Coach Lewis spent $144 for 16 sandwiches and 12 beverages for his team. Coach Walsh spent $120 for 12 sandwiches and 15 beverages for his team. Each sandwich and each beverage cost the same amount. Write a system of equations that can be used to find the cost of each sandwich, s, and the cost of each beverage, b.

Answer _____

6 Gina orders 2 sheets of wallet-sized photos and 4 sheets of portrait-sized photos for $30. Rosanne orders 3 sheets of wallet-sized photos and 3 sheets of portrait-sized photos for $27. Kristina orders 1 sheet of wallet-sized photos and 5 sheets of portrait-sized photos. Each sheet of wallet-sized photos costs the same. Each sheet of portrait-sized photos costs the same. How much does Kristina pay for her photos?

Answer _____

7 The sum of two numbers is 12. The difference between the two numbers is 18.

Part A Write a system of equations to represent the statements.

Answer _____

Part B What are the two numbers?

Answer _____

8 Aiden wants to make a 32-ounce mixture of a 12% salt solution. He plans to mix a solution of 10% salt water with a solution of 20% salt water to make this. He made this table to help him find the number of ounces, x and y, of each solution he will need to mix.

	10% Salt Water	20% Salt Water	12% Salt Solution
Mixture (oz)	x	y	
Salt (oz)			

Part A Complete the table above. Then write a system of equations that can be used to find the number of ounces of the 10% solution and 20% solution that should be mixed.

If the 32-ounce mixture is 12% salt, how many ounces of that mixture are salt?

Answer _____

Part B Solve the system of equations to find the number of ounces of the 10% solution and 20% solution that should be mixed to make the 12% solution. Explain how you know.

_____

_____

_____

_____

REVIEW

Systems of Linear Equations

1 What is the solution to the system of equations shown on this coordinate plane?

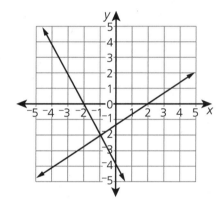

A   (–1, –2)   C   (2, 0)

B   (–2, –1)   D   (–2, 0)

2 It costs $26 for 3 bags of small beads and 4 bags of large beads. It costs $20 for 5 bags of small beads and 2 bags of large beads. Which system of equations can be used to find the cost of each size bag?

A $\begin{cases} 3x + 5y = 20 \\ 4x + 2y = 26 \end{cases}$ C $\begin{cases} 3x + 4y = 20 \\ 5x + 2y = 26 \end{cases}$

B $\begin{cases} 3x + 5y = 26 \\ 4x + 2y = 20 \end{cases}$ D $\begin{cases} 3x + 4y = 26 \\ 5x + 2y = 20 \end{cases}$

3 Is (–1, 2) a solution to this system of equations?

$$\begin{cases} -x + 2y = 3 \\ 2x - y = -4 \end{cases}$$

A   Yes. It is a solution to both equations.

B   No. It is not a solution to the first equation.

C   No. It is not a solution to the second equation.

D   No. It is not a solution to either equation.

4 How many solutions does this system of linear equations have?

$$\begin{cases} 4x = 5y + 2 \\ 4x + 5y = 2 \end{cases}$$

A   0   C   exactly 2

B   exactly 1   D   infinitely many

5 What is the solution to $\begin{cases} y = 3x - 3 \\ y = -2x + 7 \end{cases}$?

A   (0, –3)   C   (2, 3)

B   (1, 0)   D   (3, 2)

6 How many solutions are there to this system of equations? Explain how you know.

$$\begin{cases} 2x - y = 5 \\ 2x + y = 3 \end{cases}$$

_____

_____

7 What is the solution to this system of equations? Show your work.

$$\begin{cases} x - 5y = 1 \\ 2x - 7y = 8 \end{cases}$$

Answer _____

8 Graph and label this system of equations on the coordinate plane. Then identify the solution.

$$\begin{cases} y = x + 4 \\ x - y = 3 \end{cases}$$

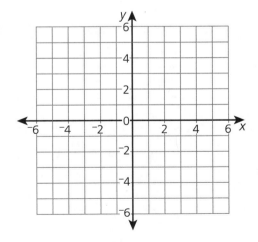

Answer _____

9 A travel agent offers the vacation packages shown in this table.

	Number of Nights in Hotel	Number of Meals	Total Cost ($)
Package A	4	8	400
Package B	6	10	580

Each hotel night costs the same. Each meal costs the same.

Part A Write a system of equations that can be used to find the cost of each hotel night and each meal in these vacation packages.

Answer _____

Part B Solve the system of equations to find the cost of each hotel night and each meal in these vacation packages. Explain how you found your answer.

_____

_____

_____

_____

10 Grady and Ted solved the system $\begin{cases} y = 3x - 5 \\ 6x - 2y = 10 \end{cases}$.

Part A Is (2, 1) a solution to this system? Explain how you know.

_____

_____

Part B Grady thinks there is only one solution to this system of equations. Ted thinks there is more than one. Who is correct, Grady or Ted? Explain how you know.

_____

_____

_____

Functions

● **Lesson 1   Function Tables** reviews what a function is and how to identify a function rule, an input value, and an output value from a function table.

● **Lesson 2 Equations of Functions** reviews how to write an equation in function notation and compares functions represented in different ways.

● **Lesson 3 Graphs of Functions** reviews how to graph a function given its equation and compares graphs of different functions.

● **Lesson 4 Linear Functions** reviews how to model situations involving linear functions and how to interpret the slope and *y*-intercept of linear functions.

Function Tables

8.F.1, 8.F.2

🏁 The variable *x* is often assigned as the input of a function. The variable *y* is often assigned as the output.

An ordered pair represents a point in a set of data or on a graph and is written in the form (*x*, *y*).

In a function, no two inputs, or *x* values, are the same.

$S = \{(3, 4)\ (5, 6)\ (7, 4)\}$

Set *S* is a function because the input values are all different. It doesn't matter if some or all output values are the same.

Look for a pattern in the input and output values to help find a function rule.

A **function** is a relationship between two sets of variables, called the **input** and the **output.** A function assigns one output for every unique input. Functions can be represented as sets of ordered pairs or in table form as a **function table.**

Which of the following sets represents a function?

Set A: {(1, 4), (2, 2), (3, 0), (2, –2), (1, –4)}

Set B:

x	1	2	3	4
y	5	5	5	5

In set A, the inputs are: 1, 2, 3, 2, 1
The outputs are: 4, 2, 0, –2, –4
These inputs are not unique since 1 and 2 appear twice, so set A is **not** a function.

In set B, the inputs, or *x*-values, are: 1, 2, 3, 4
These are all unique, so set B **is** a function.

A **function rule** describes a function. It can be used to find an output given a specific input, or to find an input given a specific output.

What function rule describes the points in this function table? Use this function rule to find *y* when *x* is 6.

x	0	1	2	3	...	6
y	8	3	–2	–7	...	

Each *x*-value in the table increases by 1. Each *y*-value in the table decreases by 5. Five is subtracted from the previous *y*-value to find the next *y*-value. The rule is "subtract 5."

To find *y* when *x* is 6, continue the pattern in the table until you reach *x* = 6.

x	3	4	5	6
y	–7	–12	–17	–22

UNIT 5 ✖✖
Functions

SAMPLE Look at this function table.

What is the input when the output is 12?

IN	OUT
–3	–2
–2	0
–1	2
0	4

A 2   **C** 4

B 3   **D** 6

The correct answer is C. First, identify a rule to describe this function. As each input increases by 1, each output increases by 2. A function rule to describe this is "add 2." Continue the pattern of adding 1 to the input and 2 to the output until you reach an output of 12: (1, 6), (2, 8), (3, 10), (4, 12). When the input is 4, the output is 12.

1 Which table does *not* represent a function?

A
x	y
1	4
2	4
3	4

C
x	y
1	1
3	3
5	5

B
x	y
2	3
2	4
2	5

D
x	y
2	6
4	4
6	2

2 Which of the following sets is a function?

A {(0, 1), (0, 2), (0, 3), (0, 4)}

B {(1, 1), (3, 2), (3, 3), (5, 4)}

C {(2, 3), (3, 1), (1, 2), (2, 1)}

D {(3, 3), (2, 2), (1, 1), (0, 0)}

3 What function rule describes this pattern?

x	2	4	6	8
y	–4	–8	–12	–16

A subtract 4 from x to get y

B subtract 6 from x to get y

C multiply x by –2 to get y

D multiply x by –4 to get y

4 What is the value of y when x is –1?

x	3	6	9	12
y	1	4	7	10

A –4   **C** –2

B –3   **D** –1

5 What is the input when the output is 10?

IN	–2	–1	0	1
OUT	0	1	2	3

A 8   **C** 12

B 9   **D** 13

SAMPLE Write a function rule to describe the data in this function table.

x	−20	−10	0	10
y	−6	4	14	24

Answer _____

    Each value of *x* and *y* increases by 10. To find the function rule, look for a pattern in the *x*- and *y*-values for each ordered pair of data. In (−20, −6), 14 is added to −20 to get −6. In (−10, 4), (0, 14), and (10, 24), the same is true. The function rule to describe this is "add 14 to *x* to get *y*."

6 In this function table, what is the output when the input is 54?

IN	9	18	27	36
OUT	6	12	18	24

Answer _____

7 The ordered pairs (*x, y*) in this table of values do **not** form a function.

IN	OUT
2	1
5	k
7	6
h	9

What could be possible values of *h* and *k*? Explain how you know.

_____

_____

_____

8 Jasper wrote this function table.

x	y
−4	−7
−3	−6
−2	−5
−1	−4

Part A Write a function rule that models this relationship.

> What pattern do you see between each ordered pair, (x, y), of data?

Answer _____

Part B What is the value of x when y = −9? Explain how you know.

_____

_____

_____

Equations of Functions

8.F.1, 8.F.2

The equation of a function can be written with other variables besides *x* and *y*.

The terms $h(x)$ and $g(x)$ are sometimes used to represent functions.

Function rules are often written as equations involving *x* and *y*. A function is linear if it has the same change in *y* for every value of *x*. Its function equation is in the form $y = mx + b$.

A function can be thought of as an input-output machine.

$$y = 2x + 55$$

Input   Output
$x = 10 \rightarrow$ $2x + 55$ $\rightarrow y = 75$

Equations are often used as function rules. You can write equations with variables such as *x* and *y* or using function notation. In **function notation,** *x* represents the inputs and $f(x)$ represents the outputs.

The equation $y = 4x - 7$ in function notation is $f(x) = 4x - 7$.
The equation $h = 20t + 75$ in function notation is $f(t) = 20t + 75$.

You can use patterns from a table to write an equation of a function.

What equation describes the values in this function table?

x	0	1	2	3
y	3	5	7	9

First write a function rule to describe this.

As the *x*-values increase by 1, the *y*-values increase by 2. This means part of the function rule is "2 multiplies *x*." Since 3 is the output when the input is 0, 3 must be added to twice the *x*-value as part of the function rule.

The function rule is "the *y*-value is 3 more than twice the *x*-value." As an equation, this is $y = 2x + 3$. In function notation, this is $f(x) = 2x + 3$.

You can also use equations of functions to make a function table.

Jorge resumes reading a book at page 55. He reads two pages every minute. The function $y = 2x + 55$ represents the page of the book, *y,* he will finish at after reading for *x* minutes. Make a table of values to find the pages he will finish at after reading for 5, 10, 20, and 30 minutes.

The *x*-values represent minutes. To find corresponding *y*-values, substitute each *x*-value into the equation and solve for *y.* Then put these values in a table.

x	5	10	20	30
y	65	75	95	115

SAMPLE Which equation matches this table of values?

x	1	2	3	4
y	1	7	13	19

A $y = x + 5$ **B** $y = x + 6$ **C** $y = 5x - 6$ **D** $y = 6x - 5$

The correct answer is D. As *x* increases by 1, *y* increases by 6. That means that 6*x* is part of the equation. Since each *y*-value is 5 less than 6 times each *x*-value, the equation is $y = 6x - 5$.

1 How is the equation $y = -4x + 1$ written in function notation?

A $f(x) = -4f + 1$ **C** $f(x) = -4y + 1$

B $f(x) = -4x + 1$ **D** $f(x) = -4f(x) + 1$

2 Which table of values matches the equation $y = -x + 3$?

A
x	y
2	-1
4	1
6	3
8	5

C
x	y
2	5
4	7
6	9
8	11

B
x	y
2	1
4	-1
6	-3
8	-5

D
x	y
2	-5
4	-7
6	-9
8	-11

3 What equation describes this table?

x	1	3	5	7
y	2	4	6	8

A $y = x + 1$ **C** $y = 2x + 1$

B $y = x + 2$ **D** $y = 2x + 2$

4 Miranda started making this table of values to show the relationship between the number of quilts she sells, *x*, and the profit, *y*, in dollars, she earns in her business.

x	1	2	3	4	5
y	?	-110	-90	-70	-50

What is the missing value in this table?

A -100   **C** -130

B -120   **D** -150

5 Which table of values models the function $f(x) = \frac{2}{3}x - 2$?

A
x	f(x)
0	-2
6	2
12	6
18	10

C
x	f(x)
0	-2
6	6
12	10
18	14

B
x	f(x)
0	-2
6	4
12	8
18	12

D
x	f(x)
0	-2
6	10
12	22
18	34

SAMPLE Write an equation that models this function table.

x	0	3	6	9
y	0	1	2	3

Answer _____

Look for a pattern that exists between each ordered pair (x, y). Each x-value increases by 3. Each y-value is $\frac{1}{3}$ each x-value. The equation that models this is $y = \frac{1}{3}x$.

6 The equation $C = 45m + 25$ models the total cost, C, in dollars, of a cell phone plan for m months. Complete this table of values to show the total cost for the first 4 months of this cell phone plan.

m				
C($)				

7 The Pierce family drives home from a vacation trip. This table of values shows the relationship between the number of gallons, g, of gasoline their car uses and the distance in miles, d, the car is from home.

g	d
1	144
2	124
3	104
4	84
5	64

Write an equation using g and d to represent the data in the table. Then write the equation in function notation.

Answer _____

8 This function table shows the relationship between the number of hours, *h*, an auto mechanic works to repair a car and the total cost, *C*, in dollars, the mechanic charges.

h	C($)
1	110
2	170
3	230
4	290

Part A Write an equation that models this relationship. Explain how you found your answer.

_____

_____

_____

_____

_____

 By what amount does *C* increase for every increase of 1 in *h*? What does this tell you about the function rule?

Part B What is the value of *C*, in dollars, when $h = 2\frac{1}{4}$? Explain how you know.

_____

_____

_____

Graphs of Functions

8.F.1, 8.F.2, 8.F.3, 8.F.5

Coordinate points are written in the form (x, y), where x is the input and y is the output.

The graph of a linear function is a straight line. The graph of a nonlinear function is a curved line.

The equation of a linear function is in the form $y = mx + b$, where m represents the slope and b represents the y-intercept of the line.

A function is increasing if it moves upward from left to right. It is decreasing if it moves downward from left to right.

A linear function is either increasing everywhere or decreasing everywhere. A nonlinear function can increase and decrease over different intervals, or values, of x.

A function represented as an equation or in table form can also be represented as a graph. The x-coordinates represent the input. The y-coordinates represent the output.

Draw the graph of $y = -2x + 1$.

Make a table of values to find coordinate points for the graph. Choose any x-value for the input and find the corresponding y-value, or output. Then plot the points on a coordinate plane.

x	y
−2	5
−1	3
0	1
1	−1
2	−3

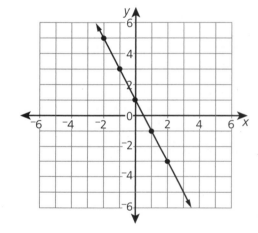

Functions can be linear or nonlinear. A **linear function** is one where it has the same change in y-values for each change in x-values. A **nonlinear function** has varying changes in x- and y-values.

Draw a graph of the function represented by this table of values. Explain whether the function is linear or nonlinear.

x	f(x)
−2	1
−1	−2
0	−3
1	−2
2	1

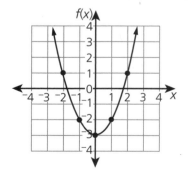

This function is nonlinear because it is not a straight line.

SAMPLE Which statement best describes the graph of this function?

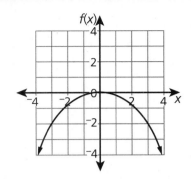

    A It increases everywhere.

    B It decreases everywhere.

    C It decreases for all values of x.

    D It increases for negative values of x.

The correct answer is D. This graph shows a nonlinear function that both increases and decreases. The graph increases for all negative values of x since it moves upward from left to right for these values. It decreases for all positive values of x since it moves downward from left to right for these values.

1 Which table of values matches this graph?

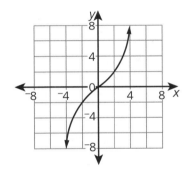

A

x	y
−2	2
−1	1
1	−1
2	−2

C

x	y
−2	−8
−1	−1
1	1
2	8

B

x	y
−2	−2
−1	−1
1	1
2	2

D

x	y
−8	−2
−1	−1
1	1
8	2

2 Functions $f(x)$ and $g(x)$ are shown below.

x	f(x)
0	9
1	6
2	3
3	0

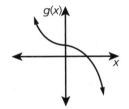

Which statement best describes these functions?

    A $f(x)$ and $g(x)$ are nonlinear.

    B $f(x)$ is nonlinear and $g(x)$ is linear.

    C $f(x)$ and $g(x)$ increase everywhere.

    D $f(x)$ and $g(x)$ decrease everywhere.

SAMPLE The function $f(x)$ is nonlinear and it increases for all
values of x. On the coordinate plane at the right,
draw a graph that could represent $f(x)$.

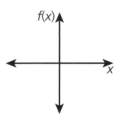

✓ A nonlinear graph is a curved line. A graph that
increases for all values of x moves upward from
left to right. The graph shown here satisfies both
of these conditions.

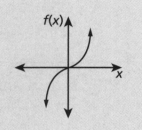

3 The function $f(x)$ is linear and it
decreases for all values of x. On
the coordinate plane at the right,
draw a graph that could represent $f(x)$.

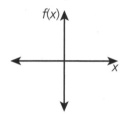

4 The surface area of a cube is represented by the function $A(s) = 6s^2$,
where s is the side length of the cube. Explain whether this function is
linear or nonlinear.

_____

_____

5 For which values of x is the function
graphed here decreasing?

Answer _____

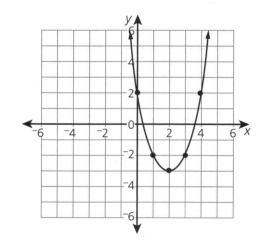

6 The function $f(x) = 0.6x$ shows the relationship between the original price, x, in dollars, and the discounted price, $f(x)$, in dollars, of all clearance items at Max's Music Store.

Part A Graph this function on the coordinate plane below.

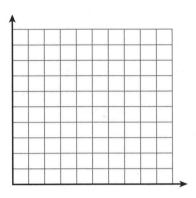

Part B The table of values below shows the relationship between the original price, x, and the discounted price, $f(x)$, of all clearance items at Timmy's Tunes.

x	20	25	30	35
$f(x)$	8	10	12	14

Find the discount factors for each store. Compare the change in $f(x)$-values to the change in x-values.

Which store has a better discount, Max's Music Store or Timmy's Tunes? Explain how you know.

_____

_____

_____

_____

Linear Functions

8.F.3, 8.F.4

A linear equation in the form $y = mx + b$ is in slope-intercept form. The slope is m and the y-intercept is b, or the point $(0, b)$.

The slope represents the rate of change. The y-intercept represents the initial value.

The slope of a line tells you how steeply a line goes up or down. Slope is the ratio of the change in y to the change in x.

A linear equation in the form $y = mx$ has a y-intercept of 0. The line intersects the origin, or center, of the coordinate graph.

The formula for the slope of a straight line through any two points (x_1, y_1) and (x_2, y_2) is
$$m = \frac{y_2 - y_1}{x_2 - x_1}$$

Everyday situations can be modeled using linear functions. Linear functions represent straight lines written in the form $y = mx + b$.

A salesperson earns a salary of $300 a week selling club memberships. He also earns $10 for every club membership he sells. Write a linear function to represent the salesperson's total weekly earnings, y, for selling x memberships.

The salesperson earns $10 for each membership sold. So, he earns $10x$ for selling x memberships. He also earns $300 each week. This amount is added to $10x$.

The linear function $y = 10x + 300$ represents this situation.

The slope and the y-intercept of a linear function tell you information about specific situations.

What do the slope and the y-intercept of the linear function above represent?

The slope is 10. This represents the amount the salesperson earns for each membership sold.

The y-intercept is 300. This represents the amount the salesperson earns each week if no memberships are sold.

You can find the slope and y-intercept of a linear function from a table of values or from a graph.

What are the slope and the y-intercept of the function below?

x	0	2	4	6
y	12	15	18	21

Pick any two points to find the slope: $m = \frac{15 - 12}{2 - 0} = \frac{3}{2}$

The y-intercept is the point $(0, b)$. Since $y = 12$ when $x = 0$, the y-intercept is $(0, 12)$.

SAMPLE Water drains from a tub. This graph shows the relationship between the time the tub drains and the amount of water remaining in the tub.

What does the slope of this line represent?

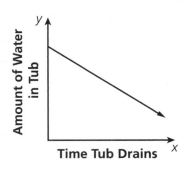

A   the rate the water drains

B   the total time it takes to drain the tub

C   the amount of water before draining

D   the amount of water left after draining

   The correct answer is A. Slope is a measure of the rate of change. In this case, it is a measure of the rate the water drains from the tub. Choice B and C are incorrect because they represent the points where the line intersects the *x*- and *y*-axes. Choice D is incorrect because when the water drains completely, the amount left in the tub is 0.

1 Which equation represents a linear function?

A $y = x^2$

C $y = x^3$

B $y = \frac{4}{x}$

D $y = \frac{3}{5}x$

2 This table shows the relationship between the total weight, *w*, in pounds, of a crate containing *t* textbooks.

t	0	8	16	24
w	4	20	36	52

What is the slope of the line that models this situation?

A   2

C   4

B $\frac{1}{2}$

D $\frac{1}{4}$

3 A catalog company charges a shipping fee of $0.25 for each pound an order weighs. A $3 handling fee is also charged. Which function represents the total fees for an order of *p* pounds?

A $f(p) = 0.25 + 3p$

B $f(p) = 0.25p + 3$

C $f(p) = 0.25(p + 3)$

D $f(p) = p(0.25 + 3)$

4 A candle is 12 inches tall. After it burns for 4 hours, it is 9 inches tall. Cam graphs the relationship between the height of the candle, *y*, and the amount of time it burns, *x*. What is the slope of the line she graphs?

A $-\frac{1}{4}$

C $-\frac{3}{4}$

B $-\frac{1}{3}$

D $-\frac{4}{3}$

SAMPLE Barry recorded the weight, in pounds, of his puppy each month for 4 months, as shown in this table.

Month	1	2	3	4
Weight	16	24	30	36

Can this puppy's weight be modeled using a linear function? Explain how you know.

Answer _____

No, it cannot. For it to be a linear relationship, the change in weight must be constant from month-to-month. During months 1 and 2, the weight change is 24 − 16 = 8 pounds. During months 2 and 3, the weight change is 30 − 24 = 6 pounds. Since these amounts are different, this is not a linear relationship.

5 This graph shows the relationship between the height of a plant, in inches, and the time, in months, that it grows.

What does the *y*-intercept of the graph represent?

Answer _____

_____

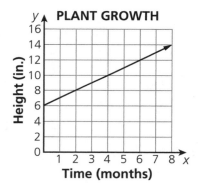

PLANT GROWTH

Height (in.) vs *Time (months)*

6 Vinny bought a backpack and some notebooks for school. The backpack cost $30. Each notebook cost $2. Write an equation to represent Vinny's total cost, *y*, for *x* notebooks.

Answer _____

7 A square with a side length of 1 foot has an area of 1 square foot. A square with a side length of 2 feet has an area of 4 square feet. Christa wrote the function $f(x) = 2x$ to represent the area of a square with a side length of *x* feet. Is this function correct?

_____

_____

8 Kayla wants to buy a new computer. She will save all the money she earns working until she can pay for it. This graph shows the relationship between the amount of time Kayla will work and the dollar amount she has left to save.

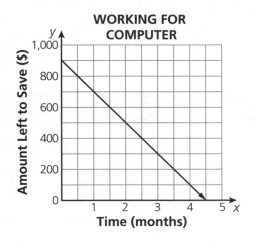

WORKING FOR COMPUTER

Amount Left to Save ($) vs. Time (months)

Part A Write the equation of the linear function that models this situation.

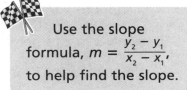

Use the slope formula, $m = \dfrac{y_2 - y_1}{x_2 - x_1}$, to help find the slope.

Answer _____

Part B What do the slope and y-intercept of this function represent?

_____

_____

_____

REVIEW

Functions

1 Which rule describes this pattern?

x	1	3	5	7
y	4	12	20	28

  A add 3 to x to get y

  B add 8 to x to get y

  C multiply x by 3 to get y

  D multiply x by 4 to get y

2 Which function is linear?

  A $f(x) = 0.2x - 5$ **C** $f(x) = x^2 + 1$

  B $f(x) = \frac{4}{x} + 3$ **D** $f(x) = x^3$

3 It costs $4 to park a car in a lot and $0.50 per hour to keep it there. Which function represents the total cost to have a car parked in this lot for h hours?

  A $f(h) = 0.5 + 4h$

  B $f(h) = 0.5h + 4$

  C $f(h) = 0.5(h + 4)$

  D $f(h) = h(0.5 + 4)$

4 What is the input when the output is 50?

IN	0	2	4	6
OUT	20	26	32	38

  A 8   **C** 12

  B 10   **D** 14

5 Which statement best describes the graph of this function?

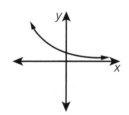

  A It increases everywhere.

  B It decreases everywhere.

  C It increases for positive values of x only.

  D It decreases for negative values of x only.

6 What equation describes this function?

x	-2	-1	0	1	2
y	4	7	10	13	16

  A $y = x + 3$ **C** $y = 3x + 10$

  B $y = x + 6$ **D** $y = -2x + 4$

7 The amount a consultant earns for traveling and each hour of work she performs is shown in this graph.

What does the *y*-intercept represent?

Answer _____

_____

8 The equation $C = 0.5m + 15$ models the total cost, C, in dollars, to rent a car and drive it m miles. Complete this table to find the total cost to rent the car for each number of miles driven.

m	100	150	200	250
C				

9 For which values of *x* is this graphed function increasing?

Answer _____

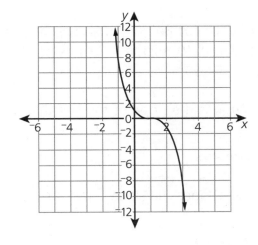

10 The function $f(x) = 2x + 10$ shows the relationship between the total cost in dollars to rent a bike, $f(x)$, and the number of hours, *x*, the bike is rented. Graph this function on the coordinate plane at the right. Be sure to label each axis and give the graph a title.

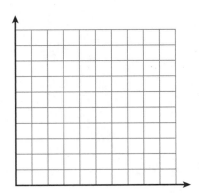

11 Look at this function table.

x	y
1	2
2	7
3	12
4	17

Part A Write an equation that models this function.

Answer _____

Part B What is the value of x when $y = 37$? Explain how you know.

_____

_____

_____

12 The cost of each call Bethany makes to her cousin from her cell phone is linear. A 10-minute call costs her $1.40. A 24-minute call costs her $2.80.

Part A What is the slope of the line that represents this situation?

Answer _____

Part B What does the slope represent?

Answer _____

Geometry, Part 1

- **Lesson 1 Translations** reviews what a translation is and the effects of translations on and off a coordinate plane.

- **Lesson 2 Reflections** reviews what a reflection is and the effects of reflections on and off a coordinate plane.

- **Lesson 3 Rotations** reviews what a rotation is and the effects of rotations on and off a coordinate plane.

- **Lesson 4 Dilations** reviews what a dilation is and the effects of dilations on a coordinate plane.

- **Lesson 5 Congruence and Similarity** reviews what congruent and similar figures are and applies translations, reflections, rotations, and dilations to these concepts.

- **Lesson 6 Angle Relationships** reviews relationships about angles, including angle sums in triangles, exterior angles of triangles, angles and parallel lines, and angles in similar triangles.

Translations

8.G.1.a, b, c; 8.G.3

A **transformation** is the movement of a geometric figure from one position to another. One type of transformation is a translation. A **translation** moves, or slides, a figure from one place to another. The size and shape of the translated figure do **not** change.

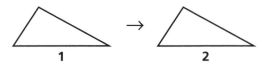

1 → 2

A translation can move a figure horizontally, vertically, or diagonally.

Image notation sometimes uses prime symbols (').

$\triangle ABC \rightarrow \triangle A'B'C'$

Figures can be translated horizontally and vertically on a coordinate plane. The translated figure is called the **image** of the original figure. Each side and angle of the original figure is **corresponding,** or matching, to the same side and angle of its image. You can use this fact to determine the amount of movement made by a translation in both directions.

Triangle *FGH* is translated to form its image, triangle *F'G'H'*, as shown. Describe this translation.

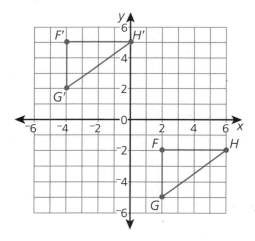

The congruent symbol (≅) shows that sides and angles are corresponding.

Translation notation is $T_{h,k}(F) = F'$ where h is the number of units moved horizontally and k is the number of units moved vertically.

The translation rule for each vertex of a figure is

$T_{h,k}(x, y) = (x + h, y + k)$

Identify corresponding sides or angles.

$\angle F \cong \angle F' \qquad \angle G \cong \angle G' \qquad \angle H \cong \angle H'$

Start at a vertex, or corner, of the original figure and count the number of places horizontally and vertically it moves to get to the corresponding vertex of its image.

Each vertex moves 6 units left and 7 units up. In translation notation, this is $T_{-6,7}(\triangle FGH) = \triangle F'G'H'$.

SAMPLE Quadrilateral *QRST* and its image *WXYZ* are shown on this coordinate plane.

Which statement is true?

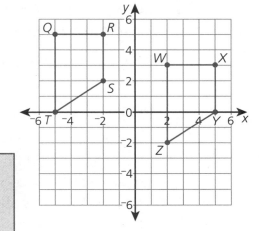

A $\overline{QR} \parallel \overline{XY}$ C $\overline{ST} \parallel \overline{XY}$

B $\overline{QR} \parallel \overline{YZ}$ D $\overline{ST} \parallel \overline{YZ}$

The correct answer is D. Find the corresponding sides for $\overline{QR}$ and $\overline{ST}$ in the image. $\overline{QR}$ corresponds to $\overline{WX}$ and $\overline{ST}$ corresponds to $\overline{YZ}$. Corresponding sides in translated figures are parallel, so $\overline{ST} \parallel \overline{YZ}$.

---

1 Which pair of figures shows a translation?

A  C

B D

2 Figure 1 translates to its image, figure 2.

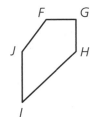 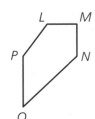

 Figure 1   **Figure 2**

Which pair of angles must be congruent?

A ∠F and ∠P   C ∠H and ∠L

B ∠F and ∠N   D ∠H and ∠N

3 Triangle *JKL* is translated according to the rule $T_{2,-5}(\triangle JKL) = \triangle J'K'L'$. The coordinates of vertex *J* are (3, 1). What are the coordinates of *J'*?

A (1, –4)   C (5, –4)

B (1, 6)   D (5, 6)

4 Which rule describes the translation from figure *P* to its image, figure *Q*?

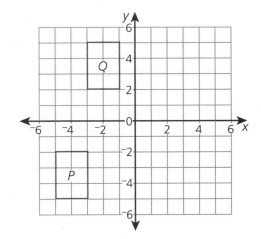

A $T_{4,2}(P) = Q$ C $T_{-2,-4}(P) = Q$

B $T_{2,7}(P) = Q$ D $T_{-2,-7}(P) = Q$

SAMPLE The coordinates of △*PQR* and its translated image, △*P'Q'R'*, are listed here.

P (3, 4) → P' (2, –2)
Q (4, 2) → Q' (3, –4)
R (5, 5) → R' (4, –1)

Write a rule to describe this translation.

Answer _____

Subtract the coordinates of the original figure from the coordinates of its image. For the *x*-coordinates: 2 − 3 = –1, 3 − 4 = –1, and 4 − 5 = –1. This shows the translation moves the triangle 1 unit left. For the *y*-coordinates: –2 − 4 = –6, –4 − 2 = –6, and –1 − 5 = –6. This shows the translation moves the triangle 6 units down. In translation notation, this is $T_{-1,-6}$(△*PQR*) = △*P'Q'R'*.

5 This diagram shows figure *ABCD* translated to form figure *A'B'C'D'*.

What is the length of side *C'D'*? Explain how you know.

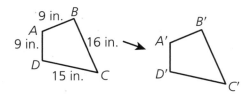

_____

_____

6 Look at the figures in problem 5. If m∠*D* is 120°, what is the measure of ∠*D'*? Explain.

_____

_____

7 Joy translated triangle *JKL* using the rule $T_{6,-8}$(△*JKL*) = △*J'K'L'* shown on this coordinate plane.

Did Joy translate the triangle correctly? Explain how you know.

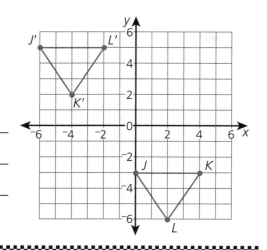

_____

_____

_____

8 Figure *HJKL* will be translated 8 units right and 4 units down to make figure *MNOP*.

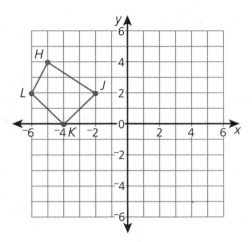

Part A Complete the statements below to show which sides of figure *MNOP* must be parallel to figure *HJKL*.

$\overline{HJ}$ ∥ _____ $\overline{JK}$ ∥ _____ $\overline{KL}$ ∥ _____ $\overline{HL}$ ∥ _____

Part B What are the coordinates of *MNOP*?
Explain how you know.

What numbers are added or subtracted from each of the original *x*- and *y*-coordinates?

_____

_____

_____

_____

Reflections

8.G.1.a, b, c; 8.G.3

A figure and its reflection are mirror images of each other.

A figure can be reflected across a horizontal line, a vertical line, or line in the form $x = k$ and $y = k$.

Prime symbols (') are sometimes used to refer to a figure's image.

$$\triangle ABC \rightarrow \triangle A'B'C'$$

A figure and its reflection are congruent.

The equation of the line representing the x-axis on a coordinate plane is $y = 0$.

The equation of the line representing the y-axis is $x = 0$.

For each vertex point (x, y) reflected across the x-axis, its image is the point $(x, -y)$.

For each vertex point (x, y) reflected across the y-axis, its image is the point $(-x, y)$.

Another type of transformation is a reflection. A **reflection** flips a figure across a line. That line is called the **line of reflection.**

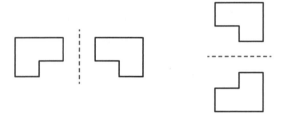

A reflected figure is the image of the original figure. The size and shape of the reflected figure does **not** change. As with translations, each side and angle of a reflected figure corresponds to the same side and angle of its original figure.

Triangle *ABC* is reflected across the line $x = 1$.

What are the coordinates of $\triangle A'B'C'$?

Draw a dotted line to represent the line of reflection, $x = 1$. Corresponding vertices of $\triangle ABC$ and its reflected image, $\triangle A'B'C'$ are the same distance from the line of reflection, just on opposite sides.

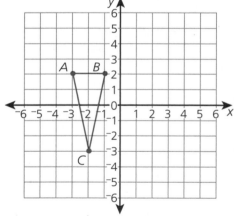

A is 4 units to the left of $x = 1$, so *A'* is 4 units to its right.

B is 2 units to the left of $x = 1$, so *B'* is 2 units to its right.

C is 3 units to the left of $x = 1$, so *C'* is 3 units to its right.

The coordinates of $\triangle A'B'C'$ are *A'* (5, 2), *B'* (3, 2), and *C'* (4, –3).

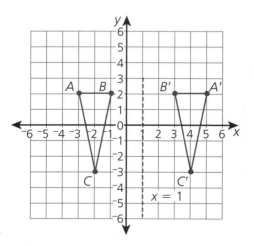

UNIT 6 ▨▨▨▨▨▨▨▨▨▨▨▨▨▨▨▨▨▨▨▨▨▨▨▨▨▨▨▨▨▨▨▨▨▨▨▨▨▨▨
Geometry, Part 1

SAMPLE Triangle *EFG* is reflected across the line $y = 0$ to form triangle *E'F'G'*.

Which statement must **not** be true?

   A $EF \cong E'F'$

   B $\angle EFG \cong \angle E'F'G'$

   C Points *E* and *E'* are the same.

   D Points *G* and *G'* are the same.

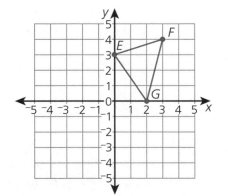

The correct answer is C. All figures and their reflected images are congruent. So, corresponding sides and corresponding angles are congruent. The line $y = 0$ represents the *x*-axis, the line of reflection. Since the point *G* lies on the *x*-axis, its image point will be the same. However, point *E'*, the image of point *E*, will be below the *x*-axis while point *E* is above it. So these two points will be different.

1 Which pair of figures shows a reflection?

   A

   C

   B

   D

2 These figures are reflections of each other.

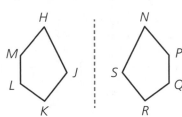

Which pair of sides must be congruent?

   A $\overline{HJ}$ and $\overline{NP}$ **C** $\overline{JK}$ and $\overline{QR}$

   B $\overline{HM}$ and $\overline{NS}$ **D** $\overline{LK}$ and $\overline{QR}$

3 Rectangle *PQRS* is reflected across a line. The image of point *Q* is at (5, –4).

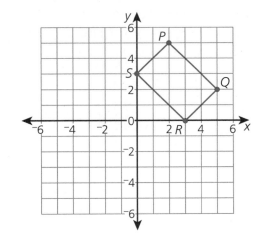

Which equation is the line of reflection?

   A $x = -1$ **C** $y = -1$

   B $x = -2$ **D** $y = -2$

SAMPLE The coordinates of △DEF and its reflected image, △D'E'F', are listed here.

Across what line was △DEF reflected?

D (3, -4) → D' (-3, -4)
E (5, -1) → E' (-5, -1)
F (1, 2) → F' (-1, 2)

Answer _____

Let the coordinates of △DEF be represented as (x, y). Then, the coordinates of △D'E'F' are represented as $(-x, y)$. This occurs when a figure is reflected across the y-axis, which is equivalent to the line $x = 0$.

4 Triangle *EFG* is reflected across the line $x = -2$. If point *E* is located at (1, 3), what are the coordinates of point *E'*?

Answer _____

5 Quadrilateral *TUVW* is reflected across the line $y = 2$.

On the same coordinate plane, draw and label quadrilateral *T'U'V'W'*, the image of quadrilateral *TUVW*.

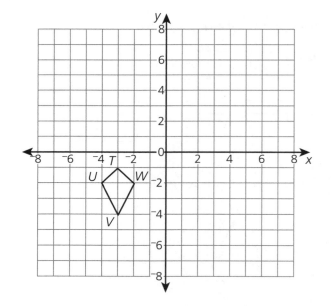

6 Lucas and Ian reflect the point (4, -3) across the y-axis. Lucas thinks the image is the point (-3, 4). Ian thinks the image is the point (-4, -3). Who is correct? Explain how you know.

_____

_____

7 Quadrilateral *FGHJ* and its reflected image are shown on this coordinate plane.

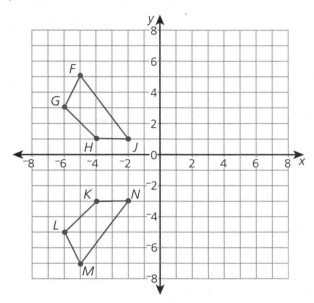

Part A Complete the statements below to show which corresponding angles in each quadrilateral are congruent.

∠*F* ≅ ∠_____   ∠*G* ≅ ∠_____   ∠*H* ≅ ∠_____   ∠*J* ≅ ∠_____

Part B Across what line was quadrilateral *FGHJ* reflected? Explain how you know.

_____

_____

_____

_____

Draw a dashed line on the grid directly between the two quadrilaterals. What equation represents this line?

Rotations

8.G.1.a, b, c; 8.G.3

Figures can be rotated any number of degrees. On a coordinate plane, figures are typically rotated either 90° or 180° in a clockwise (right) or a counterclockwise (left) direction.

On a coordinate plane, the center of rotation may be the origin, (0, 0), or any other point.

For each vertex point (x, y):

- rotated 90° clockwise about the origin, its image is the point (y, –x);

- rotated 90° counterclockwise about the origin, its image is the point (–y, x);

- rotated 180° about the origin, its image is the point (–x, –y).

A 180° clockwise rotation has the same result as a 180° counterclockwise rotation.

A third type of transformation is a rotation. A **rotation** turns a figure around a point. That point is called the **center of rotation.**

90° rotation

180° rotation

A rotated figure is the image of the original figure. The size and shape of the rotated figure does **not** change. As with translations and reflections, each side and angle of a rotated figure corresponds to the same side and angle of its original figure.

Triangle *RST* is rotated 90° counterclockwise about the origin.

What are the coordinates of *R'*, the image of point *R*?

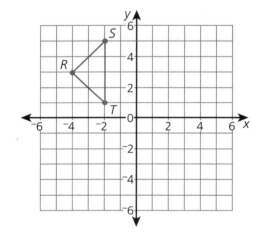

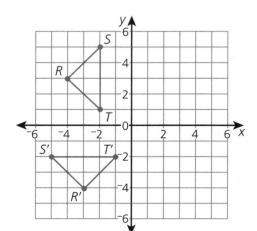

For every point with coordinates (x, y) rotated 90° counterclockwise about the origin, its image has coordinates (–y, x). So, the image of R (–4, 3) is R' (–3, –4).

UNIT 6
Geometry, Part 1

SAMPLE Rectangle *LMNP* is rotated 180° clockwise about the point (2, 1) to form *L'M'N'P'*.

What are the coordinates of *N'*?

A   (0, 4)   C   (4, 4)

B   (−4, 4)   D   (4, 0)

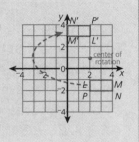

The correct answer is A. Mark the center of rotation, (2, 1), on the plane. Rectangle *LMNP* is turned halfway about this point as shown here. The location of each image point corresponds to each point of the original figure. So, the image of point has coordinates at (0, 4).

1 Which pair of triangles shows a rotation?

2 Figure 1 is rotated to form figure 2.

Figure 1   **Figure 2**

Which statement must be true?

A $\overline{HJ} \parallel \overline{MN}$ C $\overline{JK} \cong \overline{OP}$

B $\overline{HL} \parallel \overline{MP}$ D $\angle H \cong \angle M$

3 Figure P is rotated about the origin to form figure Q, as shown.

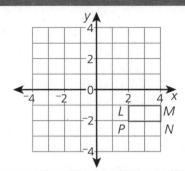

Which describes the direction of this rotation?

A   90° clockwise

B   180° clockwise

C   90° counterclockwise

D   180° counterclockwise

SAMPLE Triangle *ABC* is rotated 180° counterclockwise about the point (-4, -1) to form triangle *A'B'C'*.

Which sides of triangle *ABC* and its image, if any, are parallel?

Answer _____

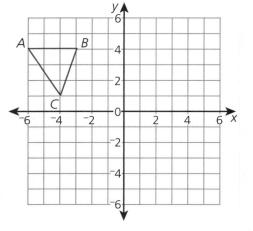

✓ Rotating a figure 180° in either direction is similar to reflecting the figure across a line. Corresponding sides of reflected figures and their images are parallel. So, corresponding sides of figures rotated 180° are parallel: $\overline{AB} \parallel \overline{A'B'}$, $\overline{BC} \parallel \overline{B'C'}$, and $\overline{AC} \parallel \overline{A'C'}$.

4 The coordinates of quadrilateral *KLMN* are *K* (4, -1), *L* (5, -4), *M* (3, -6), and *N* (2, -3). Quadrilateral *KLMN* is rotated. The coordinates of its image are *K'* (1, 4), *L'* (4, 5), *M'* (6, 3), and *N'* (3, 2). Describe this rotation, including its direction, degree measure, and center of rotation.

_____

_____

5 Triangle *TUV* is rotated 90° clockwise about the origin to form triangle *T'U'V'*.

Sara thinks the coordinates of *T'* are (2, -5). Is she correct? Explain how you know.

_____

_____

_____

_____

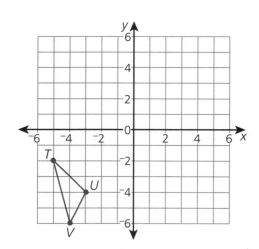

6 Triangle *PQR* is rotated 90° clockwise about point *P*.

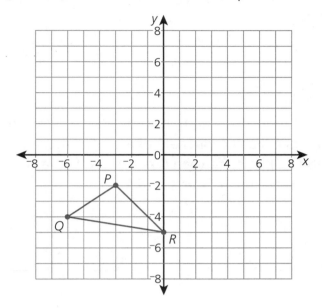

Part A   What are the coordinates of △*P'Q'R'*, the image of △*PQR*?

Try visualizing and then drawing the rotated triangle of the coordinate plane.

Answer _____

Part B   Triangle *PQR* is rotated again to form its new image, △*STU*. The coordinates of △*STU* are *S* (3, 2), *T* (6, 4), and *U* (0, 5). What degree measure, direction of rotation, and center of rotation was used to form △*STU*? Explain how you know.

_____

_____

_____

_____

Dilations

8.G.3

On a coordinate plane, the center of dilation may be the origin, (0, 0), or any other point.

A dilation is a fourth type of transformation. A **dilation** reduces or enlarges a figure. Each coordinate of a dilated figure is multiplied by a **scale factor, _k._** If _k_ is between 0 and 1, the figure is reduced. If _k_ is greater than 1, the figure is enlarged.

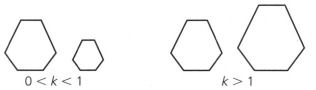

$0 < k < 1$ $k > 1$

On a coordinate plane, a dilated figure moves based on its **center of dilation.** When the center of dilation is the origin, the coordinates of each point on the original figure are multiplied by a scale factor. When the center of dilation is **not** the origin, the distance from the center of dilation to each point on the original figure is multiplied by the scale factor.

To find the distance between a center of dilation and another point, count how many units left or right and how many units up or down the point is from the center.

Rectangle _HIJK_ is dilated by a scale factor of 3 with a center of dilation at the origin. What are the coordinates of _H'I'J'K'_?

Multiply the coordinates of each point by the scale factor, 3.

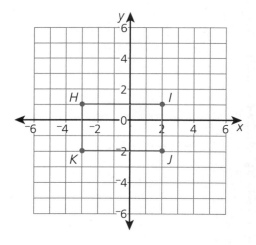

Angle measures in similar figures are the same. Side lengths in similar figures are multiplied by a scale factor and are in proportion.

$H = (-3, 1)$, so $H' = (-9, 3)$.
$I = (2, 1)$, so $I' = (6, 3)$.
$J = (2, -2)$, so $J' = (6, -6)$.
$K = (-3, -2)$, so $K' = (-9, -6)$.

A dilated figure is **similar,** but not congruent, to the original figure. The shape of the dilated figure does not change, but its size does. You can find the scale factor used to dilate a figure if you know the lengths of a pair of proportional sides. Likewise, you can find the lengths of a dilated triangle if you know the scale factor.

To solve a proportion, cross multiply.

$$\frac{x}{4} = \frac{5}{20}$$

$20x = 20$ $x = 1$

SAMPLE Triangle *TVW* was dilated by a scale factor of $\frac{3}{2}$ to form triangle *XYZ*.

What is the length of $\overline{YZ}$?

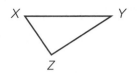

A $7\frac{1}{2}$ units   **B** $9\frac{1}{2}$ units   **C** 10 units   **D** 12 units

The correct answer is D. To find the length of $\overline{YZ}$, first identify its corresponding side on triangle *TVW*: side *YZ* corresponds to side *VW*, which is 8 units long. Then multiply the length of that side by the scale factor: $8 \times \frac{3}{2} = 12$. Side *YZ* is 12 units long.

1 Which pair of figures shows a dilation?

A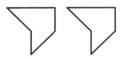

B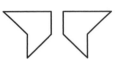

C

D

2 The coordinates to △*HJK* are *H* (8, –4), *J* (–2, 6), and *K* (0, 8). Triangle *HJK* is dilated by a scale factor of $\frac{3}{4}$ centered at the origin. What are the coordinates of the image of point *H*?

A (6, –4)   **C** (6, –2)

B (6, –3)   **D** (6, –1)

3 This coordinate plane shows the result of a dilation of △*LMN* centered at the origin.

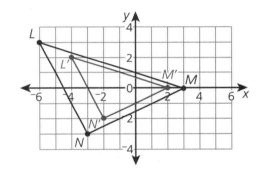

What scale factor was used for this dilation?

A $\frac{2}{3}$ **C** $\frac{3}{2}$

B $\frac{3}{4}$ **D** $\frac{4}{3}$

4 Figure *QRST* is dilated by a scale factor of 3 to form figure *Q'R'S'T'*. Which statement must be true?

A $m\angle Q = 3m\angle Q'$ **C** $ST = 3 \cdot S'T'$

B $m\angle Q = \frac{1}{3}m\angle Q'$ **D** $ST = \frac{1}{3} \cdot S'T'$

SAMPLE Quadrilateral *CDEF* is dilated by a scale factor of $\frac{1}{2}$ with center *E*.

What are the coordinates of *C'*?

Answer _____

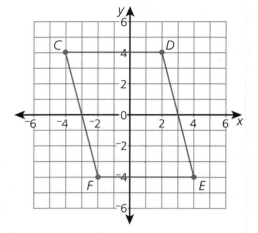

 For dilations not centered at the origin, the distance from the center of dilation to each point in the figure is multiplied by the scale factor. The distance from point *E* to point *C* is 8 units to the left and 8 units up. So, $\frac{1}{2}$ this distance is 4 units to the left from point *E* and 4 units up. This is the point (0, 0).

5 Use the figure in the sample above. After the dilation, what will be the coordinates of point *F'*? Show your work.

Answer _____

6 Figure *A'B'C'D'* is a dilation of figure *ABCD*.

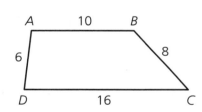   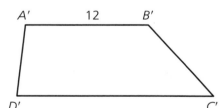

What is the length, in units, of $\overline{B'C'}$?

Answer _____

7 Harvey multiplies the coordinates of a figure by a scale factor of $\frac{3}{4}$. Is the resulting image larger than or smaller than the original? Explain.

_____

_____

8 Triangle *NOP* is dilated by a scale factor of $\frac{3}{2}$ centered at point *P*.

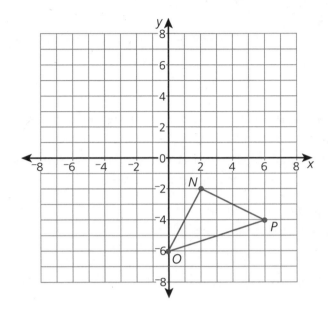

Part A What are the coordinates of △*N'O'P'*, the image of △*NOP*?

Answer _____

Part B Explain how you know.

_____

_____

_____

_____

How is finding the image points of a dilated figure with a center at (0, 0) different from finding the image points of a dilated figure with a center at another point?

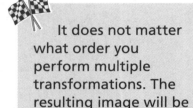

Congruency and Similarity

8.G.2, 8.G.4

It does not matter what order you perform multiple transformations. The resulting image will be the same.

Corresponding sides and corresponding angles of congruent figures are also congruent.

Corresponding angles of similar figures are congruent.

Corresponding sides of similar figures are in proportion.

Some multiple transformations may be performed using only one transformation.

Congruent figures have the same shape and size. A figure that is transformed by a translation, reflection, or rotation is congruent to its resulting image. A figure that is transformed in more than one of these ways is also congruent to its image.

Triangle *EFG* is reflected across the *x*-axis and then translated 7 units right to form △*HIJ*.

Which side of *HIJ* is congruent to side *EF*?

Triangles *EFG* and *HIJ* are congruent since a reflected triangle and a translated triangle are always congruent to the original triangle. The side of △*HIJ* that corresponds to $\overline{EF}$ is $\overline{IJ}$.

So, $\overline{EF} \cong \overline{IJ}$.

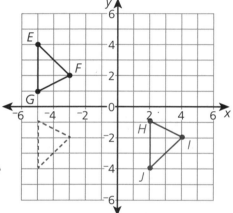

Similar figures have the same shape but are different sizes. A figure that is transformed by a dilation is similar to its resulting image. Any multiple-step transformation that involves at least one dilation will result in similar figures.

Figure 1 is transformed to form figure 2.

Figure 1   Figure 2

Describe the transformation or transformations used.

Figure 2 is larger than figure 1, so one transformation used was a dilation. Figure 2 also shows figure 1 rotated 90° counterclockwise.

SAMPLE Jill transformed rectangle *LMNO*, shown on this coordinate plane, using two steps.

The first step was a reflection across the *y*-axis. What was the second step?

A   a translation 2 units down

B   a translation 5 units down

C   a reflection across the *x*-axis

D   a reflection across the *y*-axis

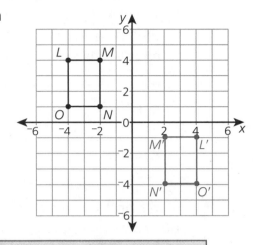

The correct answer is B. The first step results in point *L* moving to (4, 4). After the second step, *L'* is at (4, –1). To get to that point, the rectangle needs to be translated 5 units down. It may look like the rectangle was reflected across the *x*-axis, but then the coordinates of *LMNP* would not match the coordinates of its image.

1 The image of figure 1 is figure 2.

Figure 1   **Figure 2**

Which statement is true?

A $\angle Q \cong \angle W$ C $\angle R \cong \angle X$

B $\angle Q \cong \angle X$ D $\angle R \cong \angle Y$

2 Kumar transforms a figure by reflecting it over the *x*-axis and then dilating it by a scale factor of 3. What must be true of the image and the original?

A   They are congruent but not similar.

B   They are similar but not congruent.

C   They are both congruent and similar.

D   They are neither congruent nor similar.

3 Triangle *QRS* is rotated 90° clockwise and dilated by a factor of 0.5 centered on the origin.

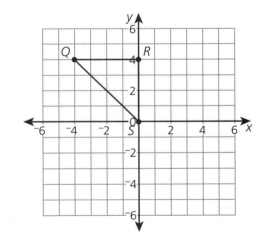

What are the coordinates of *Q'*?

A   (–2, –2)   C   (2, –2)

B   (2, 2)   D   (–2, 2)

SAMPLE Triangle *NOP* is rotated 180° clockwise about the origin. Then it is translated 2 units right and 3 units up to form its image.

What are the coordinates of the image of point *N*?

Answer _____

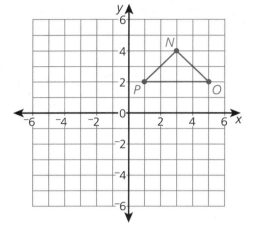

✓ First find the result for point *N* after the 180° rotation. Since *N* is at (3, 4), after the rotation, it is at (–3, –4). From that point, move 2 units right and 3 units up. The result is (2 + –3, 3 + –4) = (–1, –1). So, *N*′ = (–1, –1).

4 Use the figure in the sample above. After the transformation, what will be the coordinates of the image of point *P*?

Answer _____

5 Triangle *ABC* is dilated by a factor of 2 centered at point *A*. Then it is reflected across the *x*-axis to form △*A′B′C′*.

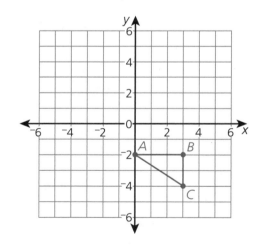

On the coordinate plane above, draw and label △*A′B′C′*.

6 Figure 1 is transformed using two steps to form figure 2, as shown on this coordinate plane.

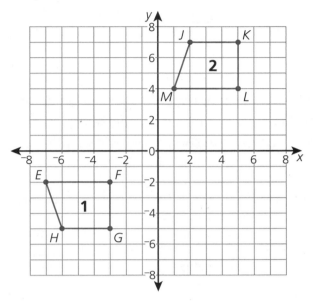

Part A Complete the statements below to show which corresponding sides in each figure are congruent.

$\overline{EF} \cong$ _____ $\overline{FG} \cong$ _____

$\overline{GH} \cong$ _____ $\overline{HE} \cong$ _____

It may help to look at the angles in each figure as well. Which pair of angles appears congruent in each figure?

Part B Describe the two steps used to complete this transformation.

_____

_____

_____

Angle Relationships

8.G.5

Interior angles are the angles inside a set of lines or segments.

Exterior angles are the angles outside a set of lines or segments.

Triangles that are translated, reflected, or rotated are congruent.

All corresponding angles in similar triangles are congruent.

Lines that do not intersect are **parallel**.

Corresponding angles are nonadjacent angles that are in the same position along a transversal.

Vertical angles are the angles opposite each other when a pair of lines intersects.

Corresponding angles, vertical angles, alternate interior angles, and alternate exterior angles are congruent on parallel lines intersected by a transversal.

Many relationships exist between angles, including angles in a triangle. The sum of the interior angles in a triangle equals 180°. You can see in the diagram below, the sum of the angles in a triangle, 3, 2, and 1, form a straight line. All straight lines measure 180°.

The triangle in position A is rotated to form the triangle in position B.

The triangle in position A is translated to form the triangle in position C.

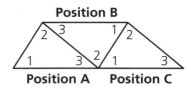

The sum of the exterior angles of a triangle equals 360°.

Two triangles are similar if two pairs of corresponding angles are congruent. This is known as **angle-angle similarity.**

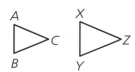

In this diagram, $\angle A \cong \angle X$ and $\angle B \cong \angle Y$. Show that $\triangle ABC$ is similar to $\triangle XYZ$ ($\triangle ABC \sim \triangle XYZ$).

The angles in a triangle sum to 180°.
$m\angle C = 180° - (m\angle A + m\angle B)$ and $m\angle Z = 180° - (m\angle X + m\angle Y)$, so $\angle C \cong \angle Z$. Therefore, $\triangle ABC \sim \triangle XYZ$.

Many types of congruent angles are formed when parallel lines are cut by a line, or **transversal.**

In this diagram, lines m and n are parallel. Line l is a transversal.

Which angles are congruent?

Corresponding angles: 1 and 5, 2 and 6, 3 and 7, 4 and 8
Vertical angles: 1 and 4, 2 and 3, 5 and 8, 6 and 7
Alternate interior angles: 3 and 6, 4 and 5
Alternate exterior angles: 1 and 8, 2 and 7

Angles 1, 4, 5, and 8 are congruent to each other.
Angles 2, 3, 6, and 7 are congruent to each other.

SAMPLE Look at this diagram.

What is the measure of ∠TVU?

A   55°   C   75°

B   65°   D   85°

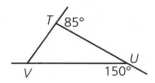

 The correct answer is A. Find the exterior angle measure by ∠TVU. Since the sum of the exterior angles is 360°, it is 360° − 85° − 150° = 125°. A line is formed by each pair of interior and exterior angles, so their sum equals 180°. The measure of ∠TVU = 180° − 125° = 55°.

1 In the diagram below, lines *p* and *q* are parallel.

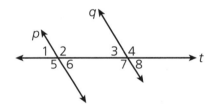

Which angles must be congruent to ∠3?

A   8 only

B   1, 6, and 8 only

C   1, 2, 4, and 8 only

D   2, 6, 7, and 8 only

2 In triangle *QRS*, the measure of ∠Q is 45° and the measure of ∠S is 18°. What is the measure of ∠R?

A   27°   C   117°

B   63°   D   153°

3 Triangle *EFG* is dilated to form △*LMN*. The measure of ∠F equals the measure of ∠M.

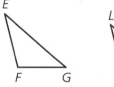

Which statement must be true to prove these two triangles are similar?

A   *EF* = *LM*

B   *EG* = *LM*

C   m∠G = m∠N

D   m∠F = m∠L + m∠N

4 In the diagram below, lines *j* and *k* are parallel.

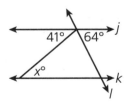

What is the value of *x*?

A   41   C   75

B   64   D   87

SAMPLE Explain why the sum of the exterior angles in a triangle equals 360°. Draw a figure to illustrate your explanation.

Answer _____

Draw any triangle. Extend the line segments forming each side of the triangle in the same direction. Cut the exterior angles out and place them together. The three angles form the angle around a point, which is equal to 360°.

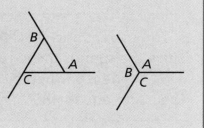

5 What is the measure of ∠Q in the figure below?

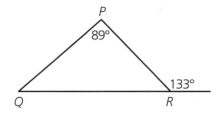

Answer _____

6 In the diagram below, ∠D ≅ ∠G and ∠E ≅ ∠H.

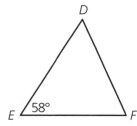
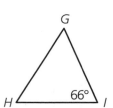

What is the measure of ∠D?

Answer _____

Read each problem. Write your answer to each part.

7 In the figure below, m∠2 = 118° and m∠5 = 72°.

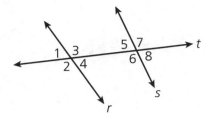

Part A Name a pair of corresponding angles.

Answer _____

Part B Are lines *r* and *s* parallel? Explain how you know.

_____

_____

_____

_____

> 🏁 What must be true of m∠6 if the lines are parallel?

8 Triangle *XYZ* and its exterior angles are shown below.

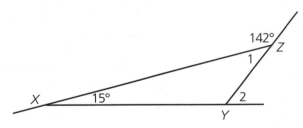

Part A What is m∠1?

Answer _____

Part B What is m∠2? Explain how you found your answer.

_____

_____

_____

REVIEW

Geometry, Part 1

Read each problem. Circle the letter of the best answer.

1 Which pair of figures shows a reflection?

A

C

B

D

2 Figure *FGHJ* was dilated by a scale factor of *k* centered at point *H*, as shown.

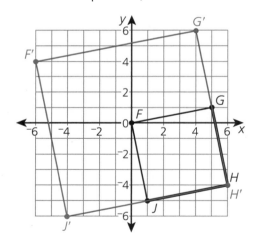

What is the value of *k?*

A $\frac{1}{4}$

C 2

B $\frac{1}{2}$

D 4

3 Figure 1 is transformed to form figure 2.

Figure 1   **Figure 2**

Which statement must be true?

A   All corresponding sides are parallel.

B   All corresponding angles are congruent.

C   Only one pair of corresponding sides are parallel.

D   Only one pair of corresponding angles are congruent.

4 Triangle *JKL* is dilated to form △*MNP*.

Which of the following must be true to prove these two triangles similar?

A   ∠*J* ≅ ∠*K* and ∠*J* ≅ ∠*L*

B   ∠*J* ≅ ∠*M* and ∠*L* ≅ ∠*P*

C $\overline{JK} \cong \overline{KL}$ and $\overline{MN} \cong \overline{NP}$

D $\overline{JK} \cong \overline{MN}$ and $\overline{KL} \cong \overline{NP}$

5 Figure *QRST* is translated according to the rule $T_{-4,-2}(QRST) = Q'R'S'T'$.
The coordinates of vertex *Q* are (–3, –2). What are the coordinates of *Q'*?

Answer _____

6 Figure *MNPQ* is transformed as shown on the coordinate plane here.

Describe this transformation in words.

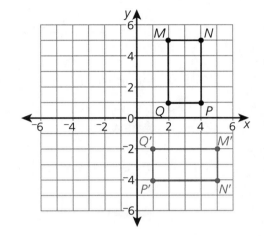

_____

_____

_____

_____

_____

7 Triangle *ABC* is reflected across the line *y* = 1. Then it is translated 2 units left to form its image.

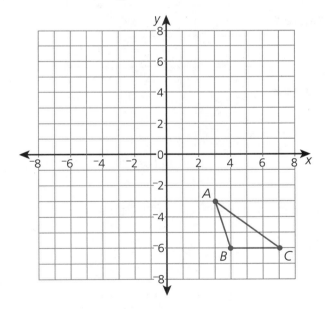

What are the coordinates of △*A'B'C'*, the image of △*ABC*?

Answer _____

8 Lines *v* and *w* are parallel in the diagram below.

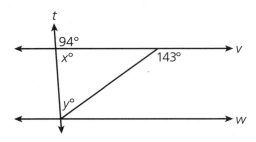

Part A What is the value of *x*?

Answer _____

Part B What is the value of *y*?

Answer _____

9 Figure 1 is transformed using two steps to form figure 2, as shown on this coordinate plane.

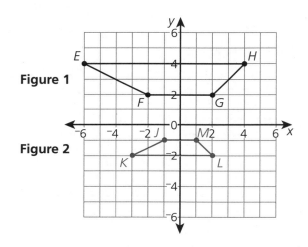

Part A Which angle in figure 2, if any, is congruent to ∠*H* in figure 1?

Answer _____

Part B Describe the two steps used to complete this transformation.

_____

_____

_____

UNIT 7

Geometry, Part 2

- **Lesson 1 Proving the Pythagorean Theorem** reviews how to prove the Pythagorean Theorem using more than one method.

- **Lesson 2 Applying the Pythagorean Theorem** reviews how to use the Pythagorean Theorem and its converse to find missing side lengths of right triangles.

- **Lesson 3 Finding Distance Between Points** reviews how to use the Pythagorean Theorem on a coordinate plane to find the distance between two points.

- **Lesson 4 Volume of Solid Figures** reviews how to solve problems involving the volumes of cones, cylinders, and spheres.

Proving the Pythagorean Theorem

8.G.6

The Pythagorean theorem

$$a^2 + b^2 = c^2$$

The Pythagorean theorem applies **only** to right triangles, not to acute or obtuse triangles.

The **legs** of a right triangle are the two shorter sides. The **hypotenuse** is the longest side.

A **Pythagorean triple** is a set of three whole numbers that can be the side lengths of a right triangle.

The side lengths 3, 4, and 5 are a Pythagorean triple since $3^2 + 4^2 = 5^2$.

You can use the Pythagorean theorem to verify if a triangle is a right triangle.

If $a^2 + b^2 = c^2$, then it is a right triangle. If $a^2 + b^2 < c^2$ or if $a^2 + b^2 > c^2$, then it is **not** a right triangle.

The **Pythagorean theorem** states that in a right triangle, the sum of the squares of the lengths of the legs equals the square of the length of the hypotenuse. It can be used to find missing side lengths of right triangles.

Many proofs have been discovered to verify the Pythagorean theorem.

Here is a right triangle with sides $a = 3$ units, $b = 4$ units, and $c = 5$ units. Use this to show the Pythagorean theorem is true.

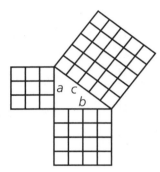

$a^2 = 9$ square units, represented by the square on the left.
$b^2 = 16$ square units, represented by the square on the bottom.
$c^2 = 25$ square units, represented by the square to the right.

Since $9 + 16 = 25$, $a^2 + b^2 = c^2$.

Here is another proof of the Pythagorean theorem.

The two squares below have equal areas. How can you use this fact to prove the Pythagorean theorem?

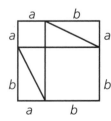   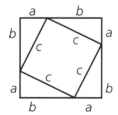

Area $= a^2 + 4\left(\frac{1}{2}ab\right) + b^2$ Area $= 4\left(\frac{1}{2}ab\right) + c^2$

Since the areas are equal, $a^2 + 4\left(\frac{1}{2}ab\right) + b^2 = 4\left(\frac{1}{2}ab\right) + c^2$.

Subtracting $4\left(\frac{1}{2}ab\right)$ from both sides gives $a^2 + b^2 = c^2$.

SAMPLE Which measures could be sides of a right triangle?

    A 4 cm, 5 cm, 6 cm   **C** 5 cm, 10 cm, 12 cm

    B 4 cm, 6 cm, 10 cm   **D** 5 cm, 12 cm, 13 cm

> The correct answer is D. Substitute each of the side lengths into the Pythagorean theorem to see which produces a true equation. Choice A: $4^2 + 5^2 \overset{?}{=} 6^2 \rightarrow 16 + 25 \overset{?}{=} 36 \rightarrow 41 \neq 36$. Choice B: $4^2 + 6^2 \overset{?}{=} 10^2 \rightarrow 16 + 36 \overset{?}{=} 100 \rightarrow 52 \neq 100$. Choice C: $5^2 + 10^2 \overset{?}{=} 12^2 \rightarrow 25 + 100 \overset{?}{=} 144 \rightarrow 125 \neq 144$. Choice D: $5^2 + 12^2 \overset{?}{=} 13^2 \rightarrow 25 + 144 \overset{?}{=} 169 \rightarrow 169 = 169$. So, only the triangle in choice D is a right triangle.

1 Look at these triangles.

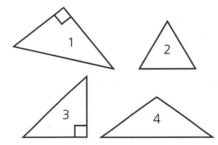

For which triangles can the Pythagorean theorem be proved?

    A 3 only   **C** 1, 2, and 3 only

    B 1 and 3 only   **D** 1, 2, 3, and 4

2 Chuck draws a triangle with side lengths of 8 inches and 11 inches. Which expression represents the area of a square drawn on the hypotenuse of this triangle?

    A $\sqrt{8 + 11}$ **C** $\sqrt{64 + 121}$

    B $8 + 11$ **D** $64 + 121$

3 This diagram shows squares 1, 2, and 3 formed from the sides of a right triangle.

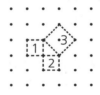

Which statement explains how each square is related?

    A area of square 1 + area of square 2 = area of square 3

    B area of square 1 × area of square 2 = area of square 3

    C length of square 1 + length of square 2 = length of square 3

    D length of square 1 × length of square 2 = length of square 3

4 Which of the following sets of side lengths is a Pythagorean triple?

    A 9, 16, 25   **C** 24, 32, 40

    B 12, 15, 20   **D** 32, 42, 52

SAMPLE Here is part of a proof of the Pythagorean theorem that uses the figure below.

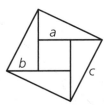

$$c^2 = (a - b)^2 + \underline{\quad ? \quad}$$
$$c^2 = a^2 - 2ab + b^2 + \underline{\quad ? \quad}$$
$$c^2 = a^2 + b^2$$

The same expression is missing from the first two equations. What is the expression?

Answer _____

The first equation in the proof shows that the total area of the large square, c^2, is equal to the sum of the shapes inside the square. The area of the small inside square is $(a - b)^2$. The area of each right triangle inside the square is $\frac{1}{2}ab$. The expression missing from the equations is the sum of the 4 right triangles, $4 \times \frac{1}{2}ab = 2ab$.

5 Is the triangle shown here a right triangle?

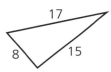

Explain how you know.

_____

_____

6 A triangle has side lengths of 21, 28, and 35 units. Chloe says these numbers are Pythagorean triples, so the triangle must be a right triangle. Without finding the squares, how can you determine if Chloe is correct? Explain.

_____

_____

7 Triangles *P* and *Q* are shown below.

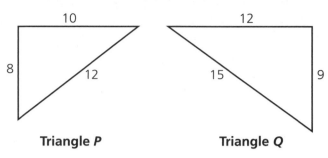

Triangle *P*   **Triangle *Q***

Part A   Complete this table for triangles *P* and *Q*.

Triangle	Length of First Leg	Square of First Leg	Length of Second Leg	Square of Second Leg	Length of Hypotenuse	Square of Hypotenuse
P						
Q						

Part B   Which of these two triangles, *P* and *Q*, are right triangles? Explain how you know.

What does the Pythagorean theorem state about the side lengths of a right triangle?

_____

_____

_____

_____

_____

Applying the Pythagorean Theorem

8.G.6, 8.G.7

The Pythagorean theorem

$$a^2 + b^2 = c^2$$

You can use a calculator to approximate the values of square roots that are not perfect squares.

$\sqrt{61} = 7.810249... \approx 7.8$

The **converse of the Pythagorean theorem** states that if $a^2 + b^2 = c^2$, then there exists a right triangle with legs a and b and hypotenuse c.

A **right triangle** is a triangle with exactly one 90°, or right, angle.

An **acute triangle** is a triangle with all angles between 0° and 90°.

An **obtuse triangle** is a triangle with exactly one angle between 90° and 180°.

The Pythagorean theorem can be used to solve problems involving the sides of right triangles.

A television screen is 36 inches long and 24 inches tall.

What is the approximate value of d, the length of the diagonal of the screen?

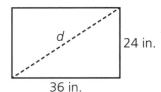

Substitute the given lengths as the legs of a right triangle and solve for the hypotenuse in the Pythagorean theorem.

$$a^2 + b^2 = c^2$$
$$36^2 + 24^2 = c^2$$
$$1,296 + 576 = c^2$$
$$1,872 = c^2 \text{ so } \sqrt{1,872} = c \approx 43.3 \text{ inches}$$

The diagonal is 43.3 inches.

The converse of the Pythagorean theorem can be used to describe the angles in a triangle based on its side lengths.

For any triangle with side lengths a, b, and c:

- if $a^2 + b^2 = c^2$, then it is a right triangle.
- if $a^2 + b^2 > c^2$, then it is an acute triangle.
- if $a^2 + b^2 < c^2$, then it is an obtuse triangle.

Triangle *ABC* has side lengths of 9 mm, 15 mm, and 18 mm. What type of triangle, based on its angles, is *ABC*?

Apply the converse of the Pythagorean theorem.

Substitute the given values for a, b, and c.

$$9^2 + 15^2 \stackrel{?}{=} 18^2$$
$$81 + 225 \stackrel{?}{=} 324$$
$$306 < 324$$

Triangle *ABC* is obtuse since $a^2 + b^2 < c^2$.

Read each problem. Circle the letter of the best answer.

SAMPLE A 20-foot ladder rests against a wall. The bottom of the ladder is 8 feet from the base of the wall.

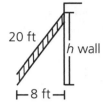

Approximately how high up the wall does the top of the ladder reach?

A 12 ft   **B** 18 ft   **C** 22 ft   **D** 28 ft

The correct answer is B. Here you know the length of a leg and the hypotenuse. To find the length of the other leg, first substitute the known values into the Pythagorean theorem, $a^2 + b^2 = c^2$: $8^2 + b^2 = 20^2$. Then work backward: $64 + b^2 = 400$, $b^2 = 336$, $b = \sqrt{336} = 18.33... \approx 18$ ft.

---

1 Which of the following represents the side lengths of an acute triangle?

A 2 m, 3 m, 4 m   **C** 4 m, 5 m, 6 m

B 2 m, 3 m, 5 m   **D** 4 m, 5 m, 7 m

2 A gift box has a square base with a length of 30 cm. What is the approximate length of the diagonal of the base of the gift box?

A 30.4 cm   **C** 54.4 cm

B 42.4 cm   **D** 60.4 cm

3 A rectangular field is 100 m long and 75 m wide. Fay walked diagonally across the field from one corner to the opposite. What distance did Fay walk?

A 125 m   **C** 150 m

B 135 m   **D** 175 m

4 A wire is tied to the trunk of a tree for support, as shown in this diagram.

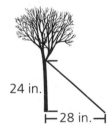

24 in.

28 in.

What is the approximate length of the wire?

A 26 in.   **C** 35 in.

B 32 in.   **D** 37 in.

5 This diagram shows the locations of three cities on a map.

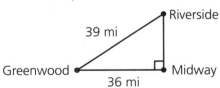

How far apart are Midway and Riverside?

A 3 mi   **C** 15 mi

B 6 mi   **D** 25 mi

SAMPLE How many right angles, acute angles, and obtuse angles are in a triangle with sides measuring 12 cm, 16 cm, and 20 cm?

Answer _____

> Substitute these values for a, b, and c into the Pythagorean theorem: $12^2 + 16^2 \stackrel{?}{=} 20^2 \rightarrow 144 + 256 \stackrel{?}{=} 400 \rightarrow 400 = 400$. So this is a right triangle. All right triangles have exactly one right angle and two acute angles. There are no obtuse angles in a right triangle.

6 A bridge goes across a river, as shown in this diagram.

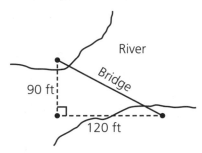

What is the length, in feet, of the bridge?

Answer _____

7 A rectangular mirror has a length of 24 inches and a diagonal that measures 30 inches. Can the width of this mirror be 16 inches? Explain how you know.

_____

_____

_____

8 This diagram shows a kite and its frame. The values *a* and *b* represent the lengths of the legs of a lower triangle formed inside the kite.

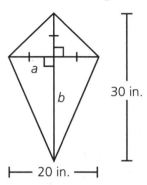

30 in.

20 in.

Part A What are the values of *a* and *b?*

Answer *a* = _____ *b* = _____

Part B What is the perimeter, to the nearest inch, of the kite? Explain how you know.

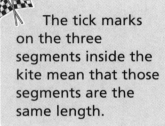

The tick marks on the three segments inside the kite mean that those segments are the same length.

_____

_____

_____

Finding Distance Between Points

8.G.8

The Pythagorean theorem

$a^2 + b^2 = c^2$

The value of c in $a^2 + b^2 = c^2$ is $c = \sqrt{a^2 + b^2}$.

The length AB equals $\sqrt{4^2 + 3^2}$.

The **distance formula** is a way to find the distance between two points.

For any two points (x_1, y_1) and (x_2, y_2), the distance between them is $\sqrt{(x_1 - x_2)^2 + (y_1 - y_2)^2}$

You can think of a and b, the legs of a right triangle, as $a = (x_1 - x_2)$ and $b = (y_1 - y_2)$.

The Pythagorean theorem can be used to find the distance between two points.

What is the length of segment AB shown on this coordinate plane?

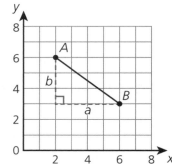

Think of $\overline{AB}$ as the hypotenuse of a right triangle with legs represented by the horizontal and vertical dashed segments. Count the number of units that make the dashed segments. Use these values in the Pythagorean theorem as the legs of the right triangle.

$a^2 + b^2 = AB^2$ $4^2 + 3^2 = AB^2$
$16 + 9 = AB^2$
$25 = AB^2$ so $AB = \sqrt{25} = 5$ units

Sometimes the horizontal and vertical distances are not easy to count. You can still find these lengths and use the Pythagorean theorem to find the distance between the points.

What is the approximate length of $\overline{MN}$?

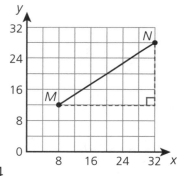

Identify the coordinates of the points: M (8, 12) and N (32, 28)

To find the length of the horizontal dashed segment, find the difference between the x-coordinates: $32 - 8 = 24$

To find the length of the vertical dashed segment, find the difference between the y-coordinates: $28 - 12 = 16$

$24^2 + 16^2 = MN^2$
$576 + 256 = MN^2$
$832 = MN^2$ so $MN = \sqrt{832} \approx 28.8$ units

SAMPLE The coordinates of $\overline{PQ}$ are P (-50, 30) and Q (30, -30).

What is the length of $\overline{PQ}$?

A   80 units   C   120 units

B   100 units   D   140 units

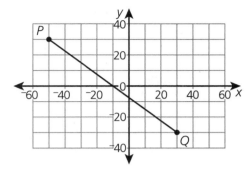

The correct answer is B. Picture this as a right triangle with hypotenuse $\overline{PQ}$ and legs a and b. Subtract the x-coordinates to find a and the y-coordinates to find b: $a = 30 + (-50) = 80$, $b = -30 - 30 = -60$. Use the Pythagorean theorem: $(80)^2 + (-60)^2 = PQ^2 \rightarrow$ $6{,}400 + 3{,}600 = PQ^2 \rightarrow 10{,}000 = PQ^2$. So, $PQ = \sqrt{10{,}000} = 100$.

1 The coordinates of $\overline{FG}$ are F (5, 7) and G (3, 11). What are the lengths of the legs of the right triangle if $\overline{FG}$ is the hypotenuse?

A   2 and 4   C   4 and 9

B   2 and 8   D   4 and 16

2 Which expression can be used to find the length of JK shown below?

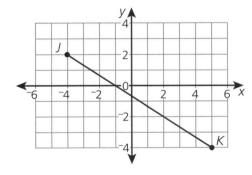

A $\sqrt{(-4 + 5)^2 + (2 + (-4))^2}$

B $\sqrt{(-4 + 5)^2 - (2 + (-4))^2}$

C $\sqrt{(-4 - 5)^2 + (2 - (-4))^2}$

D $\sqrt{(-4 - 5)^2 - (2 - (-4))^2}$

3 What is the approximate length of $\overline{RS}$ shown below?

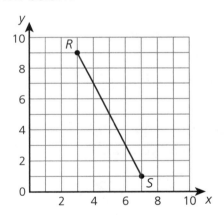

A   9 units   C   11 units

B   10 units   D   12 units

4 Line segment VW has endpoints at (6, 1) and (-6, 6). What is the length of $\overline{VW}$?

A   7 units   C   17 units

B   13 units   D   19 units

SAMPLE Which two points on this coordinate plane are $\sqrt{40}$ units apart?

Answer _____

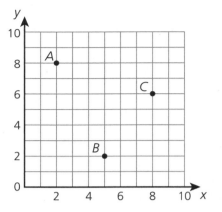

 Count the number of horizontal and vertical units between each pair of points. Then apply the Pythagorean theorem to find each length: $AB = \sqrt{3^2 + 6^2} = \sqrt{45}$, $BC = \sqrt{3^2 + 4^2} = \sqrt{25}$, $AC = \sqrt{2^2 + 6^2} = \sqrt{40}$. Points A and C are $\sqrt{40}$ units apart.

Use quadrilateral *QRST* on this coordinate plane to answer questions 5–7.

5 What is the length, in units, of $\overline{SR}$?

Answer _____

6 What is the length, to the nearest tenth unit, of $\overline{ST}$? Show your work.

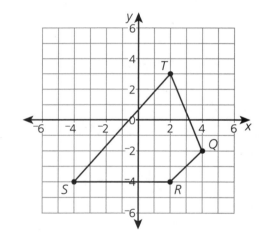

Answer _____

7 Cora used this expression to find the length of QT.

$$\sqrt{(4 - 3)^2 + (\text{-}2 - 2)^2}$$

Is this expression correct? Explain how you know.

_____

_____

8 Line segment *LM* has endpoints *L* (–15, 25) and *M* (–15, –35), as shown on this coordinate plane.

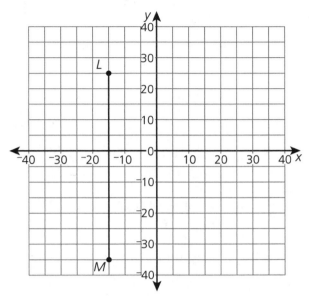

Part A What is the length of $\overline{LM}$?

Answer _____

Part B Point *N* is placed on this coordinate plane at (30, 10) to form △*LMN*. List the side lengths of △*LMN* in order from least to greatest. Explain how you found your answer.

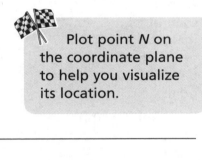

Plot point *N* on the coordinate plane to help you visualize its location.

_____

_____

_____

Volume of Solid Figures

8.G.9

Volume is measured in cubic units.

cubic inches, or in.^{3}
cubic feet, or ft^3
cubic meters, or m^3

A **cylinder** has two circular bases and a curved side.

A **cone** has one circular base and a curved side that meets at a point.

A **sphere** is a solid object made up of a set of points equal distance from a center point.

The symbol π (pi) represents the irrational number 3.141592654....

Approximations of π include 3.14 or $\frac{22}{7}$.

The diameter of a circle is twice the length of the radius.

$$d = 2r \text{ or } r = \frac{1}{2}d$$

You can use a calculator to find the square roots and cube roots of numbers.

Volume measures the amount of space inside a solid object. The formulas for the volume of some solid figures are shown below.

• $V_{\text{cylinder}} = \pi r^2 h$ volume of a cylinder with radius r and height h

• $V_{\text{cone}} = \frac{1}{3}\pi r^2 h$ volume of a cone with radius r and height h

• $V_{\text{sphere}} = \frac{4}{3}\pi r^3$ volume of a sphere with radius r

This snack canister is 10 inches tall and has a diameter of 8 inches.

What is the approximate volume of the canister?

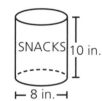

Use the formula for the volume of a cylinder: $V_{\text{cylinder}} = \pi r^2 h$

The radius is 4 inches and the height is 10 inches.

$$V_{\text{cylinder}} = \pi(4)^2(10)$$
$$= 160\pi \approx 160(3.14) = 502.4 \text{ cubic inches}$$

The volume of the canister is approximately 502.4 in.^{3}.

You can also use the volume formulas to find missing dimensions of solid objects.

The volume of a sphere-shaped ball is $4,500\pi$ cubic centimeters. How long is the radius of this ball?

Use the formula for the volume of a sphere: $V_{\text{sphere}} = \frac{4}{3}\pi r^3$

$$4,500\pi = \frac{4}{3}\pi r^3$$
$$4,500\pi \cdot \frac{3}{4\pi} = \frac{4}{3}\pi r^3 \cdot \frac{3}{4\pi}$$
$$3,375 = r^3, \text{ so } r = \sqrt[3]{3,375} = 15 \text{ centimeters}$$

The radius of the ball is 15 centimeters.

SAMPLE A decorating tip used in baking is in the shape of a cone, as shown.

What is the amount of space inside this tip?

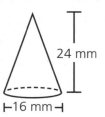
24 mm
⊢16 mm⊣

A   512π mm³   C   2,048π mm³

B   1,536π mm³   D   6,144π mm³

The correct answer is A. The formula for the volume of a cone is $V_{cone} = \frac{1}{3}\pi r^2 h$. Here, $r = 16 \div 2 = 8$ mm and $h = 24$ mm. Substitute these values into the formula to find the volume: $V = \frac{1}{3}\pi(8)^2(24) = 512\pi$. The volume is 512π cubic millimeters.

1 The radius of a spherical globe is 9 inches. What is the volume of the sphere?

A   108π in.³   C   972π in.³

B   432π in.³   D   7,776π in.³

2 A candle is in the shape of a cylinder. It is 8 cm tall and has a radius of 3 cm. What is the approximate volume of the candle?

A   75 cm³   C   602 cm³

B   226 cm³   D   1,809 cm³

3 A dome-shaped structure is in the shape of a half-sphere. The diameter of the dome is 30 yards long, as shown below.

⊢30 yd⊣

What is the volume inside the dome?

A   2,250π yd³   C   13,500π yd³

B   4,500π yd³   D   18,000π yd³

4 The cone-shaped scoop shown below has a volume of 25 cubic centimeters.

6 cm

What is the approximate length of the radius of this scoop?

A   2 cm   C   4 cm

B   3 cm   D   5 cm

5 The cylinder and cone shown below have the same volume.

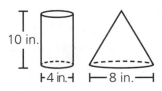
10 in.
⊢4 in.⊣   ⊢8 in.⊣

What is the height of the cone?

A $2\frac{1}{2}$ in.   C   5 in.

B   4 in.   D $7\frac{1}{2}$ in.

SAMPLE A silo is in the shape of a cylinder. When completely filled, the silo holds 1,600π cubic feet of grain. The diameter of the silo is 16 feet. What is the height, in feet, of the silo?

Answer _____

 Substitute the values of the volume and the radius into the volume formula, $V_{cylinder} = \pi r^2 h$. Remember that if the diameter is 16 feet, the radius is 8 feet: $1,600\pi = \pi(8^2)h$. Then solve to find the height: $\frac{1,600\pi}{64\pi} = h$, so $h = 25$ feet. The height of the silo is 25 feet.

6 This spherical exercise ball has a diameter of 42 centimeters.

What is the approximate volume, in cubic centimeters, of the ball? Use $\frac{22}{7}$ for π.

Answer _____

7 This cone has a volume of 2,512 cubic inches.

What is the diameter, to the nearest inch, of the cone?

24 in.

Answer _____

8 Brad used this calculation to find the volume of a cylinder with a radius of 7 centimeters and a height of 10 centimeters.

$$V_{cylinder} = \pi(2)(7)(10) = 140\pi$$

Is this calculation correct? Explain why.

_____

_____

9 A toy tower is made from a cone placed directly on top of a cylinder, as shown below.

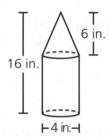

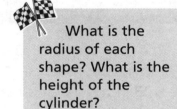
What is the radius of each shape? What is the height of the cylinder?

Part A What is the total volume, in cubic inches, of the tower? Leave your answer in terms of π.

Answer _____

Part B Explain how you found your answer.

_____

_____

_____

10 A rubber ball has a radius of 12 centimeters.

Part A What is the approximate volume, to the nearest cubic centimeter, of the rubber ball? Use 3.14 for π.

Answer _____

Part B A smaller rubber ball has radius of 6 centimeters. Joe thinks the volume of this ball is half the volume of the larger ball. Is he correct? Explain how you know.

_____

_____

_____

REVIEW

Geometry, Part 2

Read each problem. Circle the letter of the best answer.

1 The base of a cardboard moving box is rectangular. Its length is 24 inches. Its width is 18 inches. What is the length of the diagonal of the base of the moving box?

A 21 in.   **C** 36 in.

B 30 in.   **D** 42 in.

2 Which triangle is a right triangle?

A

C

B

D

3 Which of the following represents the side lengths, in units, of an obtuse triangle?

A 4, 6, 7   **C** 6, 8, 10

B 5, 6, 9   **D** 7, 9, 11

4 Which expression can be used to find the length of $\overline{RS}$ shown below?

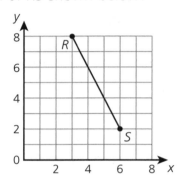

A $\sqrt{(3-6)^2 + (8-2)^2}$

B $\sqrt{(3-6)^2 - (8-2)^2}$

C $\sqrt{(8-3)^2 + (6-2)^2}$

D $\sqrt{(8-3)^2 - (6-2)^2}$

5 A mug is in the shape of a cylinder. The mug is 11 centimeters tall and has a diameter of 8 centimeters. What is the approximate volume of the mug?

A 276 cm^3 **C** 704 cm^3

B 553 cm^3 **D** 2,211 cm^3

6 A 32-foot ramp is placed on the ground 30 feet from the edge of a loading dock, as shown in this diagram.

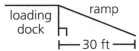

Approximately how high off the ground is the top of the ramp?

Answer _____

7 The volume of the sphere on the snow globe shown here is $\frac{9}{2}\pi$ cubic inches.

What is the radius, in inches, of the snow globe?

Answer _____

8 Tad marked the locations of his home, work, and favorite restaurant as shown in this diagram of a city map.

What is the shortest distance, in blocks, between Tad's home and work?

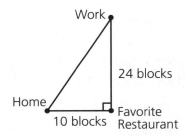

Answer _____

9 The number of small squares inside each larger square in this diagram represents the area of the larger square.

Is the triangle represented in the diagram a right triangle? Explain how you know.

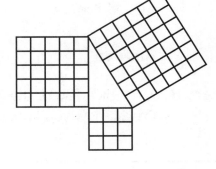

_____

_____

_____

_____

_____

10 The cone and the cylinder shown here both have a volume of
36π cubic inches.

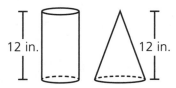

Part A What is the radius, in inches, of each object?

Answer _____

Part B Explain how you found your answer.

_____

_____

_____

11 This coordinate plane shows the placement
of colored flags along hiking trails in a park.

Each unit on the coordinate plane
represents a distance of 100 yards.

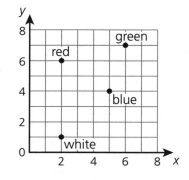

Part A What is the distance, in yards,
between the white flag and
the red flag?

Answer _____

Part B Is the blue flag or the green flag closer to the red flag?
Explain how you know.

_____

_____

_____

Statistics and Probability

● **Lesson 1 Scatter Plots** reviews how to construct and interpret scatter plots, including finding correlations between two quantities.

● **Lesson 2 Lines of Best Fit** reviews how to draw appropriate lines to fit data on scatter plots, use equations of best-fit lines to solve problems, and interpret the slope and y-intercept of a best-fit line.

● **Lesson 3 Two-Way Tables** reviews how to construct and interpret two-way tables on two categorical variables, including finding correlations between two data sets.

Scatter Plots

8.SP.1

A **linear relationship** exists when data points in a scatter plot easily surround a straight line. Otherwise, a **nonlinear relationship** exists.

Correlation describes a tendency, *not* definite cause and effect.

Data points that are in a **cluster** are closely grouped together.

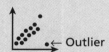
← Cluster

A data point that is set apart from most other data points is an **outlier**.

← Outlier

If data points cluster in a horizontal direction, *no correlation* exists.

If data points cluster in a vertical direction, an *undefined correlation* exists.

A **scatter plot** is a graph of plotted points that shows the relationship between two sets of data. To make a scatter plot given two sets of data, *x* and *y*, label the *x*- and *y*-axes on a coordinate plane. Then plot each point (*x*, *y*) on the plane.

Make a scatter plot to show the data in this table.

PRECIPITATION IN JENNA'S HOMETOWN

Year	1	2	3	4	5	6	7	8
Amount (in.)	8.4	9.2	8.6	8.0	7.5	6.5	6.0	5.8

Let the *x*-axis represent the year. Let the *y*-axis represent the amount of precipitation.

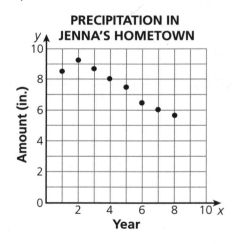

PRECIPITATION IN JENNA'S HOMETOWN

The scatter plot above shows a downward moving pattern in the amount of precipitation as the years increase. This pattern, or relationship, is known as **correlation.** Two data sets can have a positive correlation, a negative correlation, or no correlation.

Positive correlation
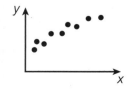

Negative correlation
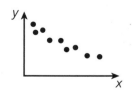

No correlation
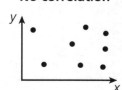

UNIT 8 :::
Statistics and Probability

SAMPLE This scatter plot shows the relationship between the average temperature at a sports stadium and bottled water sales.

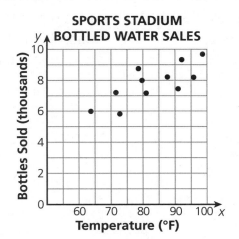

SPORTS STADIUM BOTTLED WATER SALES

Which statement best describes this relationship?

A As temperature increases, sales of bottled water tend to increase.

B As temperature increases, sales of bottled water tend to decrease.

C As temperature increases, sales of bottled water always increase.

D As temperature increases, sales of bottled water always decrease.

The correct answer is A. The data points on this graph move in a general upward direction. This means that as the temperature increases, bottled water sales tend to increase. Sales do not *always* increase as the temperature increases. For example, when temperatures were around 79°, 80°, and 81°F, bottled water sales decreased slightly as the temperature increased.

1 What type of correlation does the scatter plot show?

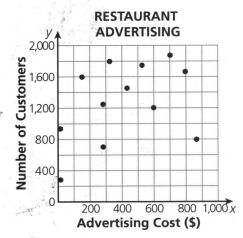

RESTAURANT ADVERTISING

A positive

B negative

C none

D undefined

2 Which scatter plot shows a nonlinear relationship between the data?

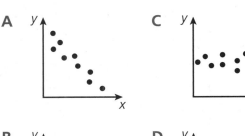

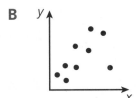

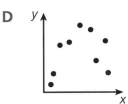

SAMPLE The data points on this scatter plot show the relationship between the scores students received on a math test and a science test.

Which data point represents an outlier?

Answer _____

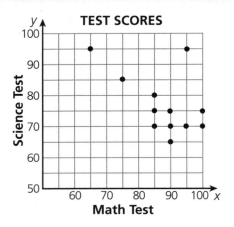

   An outlier is a point that is not near most other points on a scatter plot. It is also a point set apart from the direction most other data points follow. On this scatter plot, most data points follow a downward direction, except for the point (95, 95). This is the outlier.

3 This table shows the ages of 10 married couples that responded to a survey.

AGES OF SURVEY RESPONDERS

Husband's Age	Wife's Age
25	27
40	33
32	30
30	29
36	40
34	35
36	32
35	30
33	33
43	39

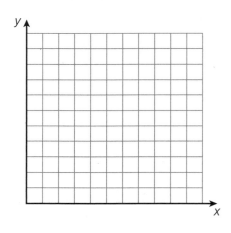

Draw a scatter plot on the coordinate plane to show the data.

4 What kind of correlation, if any, is shown by the scatter plot you made? Explain how you know.

_____

_____

Read the problem. Write your answer to each part.

5 This table shows the relationship between the approximate population of ten states and the number of representatives the state has in the House of Representatives.

STATE POPULATION AND REPRESENTATIVES

Population (millions)	Number of Representatives	Population (millions)	Number of Representatives
4.5	7	5.1	8
2.7	4	4.3	7
3.4	5	7.1	11
1.2	2	6.1	9
2.9	5	4.0	6

Part A Make a scatter plot to show the data on the coordinate plane below.

What axis does population belong on? What axis does the number of representatives belong on?

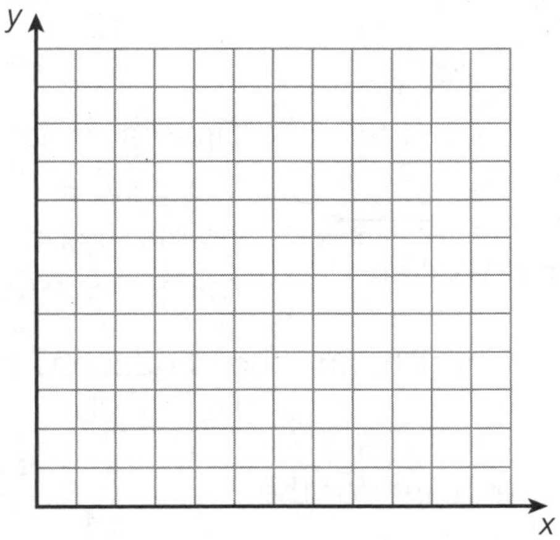

Part B What type of correlation, if any, exists between the population and the number of representatives? Explain how you know.

____

____

____

Lines of Best Fit

8.SP.2, 8.SP.3

A line of best fit does *not* connect all data points on a scatter plot. It goes between the data points to show the trend, or pattern, of the data.

A **trend line** is an approximate line of best fit. A trend line is surrounded by the data points on a scatter plot and follows the general direction of the data.

Lines of best fit are straight lines when linear relationships exist.

The general equation for a straight line is $y = mx + b$, where m represents the slope and b represents the y-intercept.

The y-intercept for this trend line, 6, represents the minimum shipping cost for any order. The slope, 0.25, represents a $0.25 charge per pound the order weighs.

A **line of best fit** is a line that goes through data points on a scatter plot. The distance between the line and all points above the line is the same as the distance between the line and all points below the line.

Draw a trend line through the data points on this scatter plot.

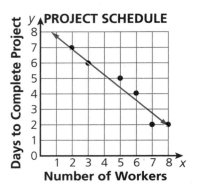

Draw a straight line that follows the general direction of the data points. It should go between as many points as possible.

You can use lines of best fit and their equations to solve problems.

The equation $y = 0.25x + 6$ represents a trend line for the data on this scatter plot.

Based on this, what is the expected shipping cost for an order that weighs 50 pounds?

The variable x represents the weight. The variable y represents the shipping cost. Substitute $x = 50$ into the equation of the trend line and solve for y.

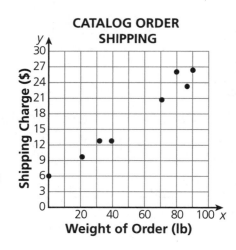

$$y = 0.25(50) + 6 = 18.50$$

The expected shipping cost for a 50-pound order would be $18.50.

SAMPLE This scatter plot with line of best fit shows the relationship between the circumference of a tree trunk and its total height.

What does the slope of this line represent?

A the beginning height of a tree

B the beginning circumference of a tree trunk

C the time it takes for the circumference to equal the height

D the amount the height increases as the circumference increases by 1

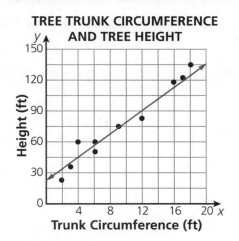

TREE TRUNK CIRCUMFERENCE AND TREE HEIGHT

Height (ft)

Trunk Circumference (ft)

 The correct answer is D. Slope is a measure of a rate of change. The slope of this line measures the rate at which the height of the tree increases as the circumference of the tree trunk increases.

1 Which scatter plot shows the best line of fit?

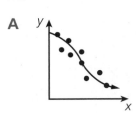

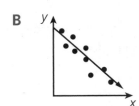

2 This scatter plot shows the relationship between the number of times a baseball player was at bat and the number of hits he made during ten seasons he played.

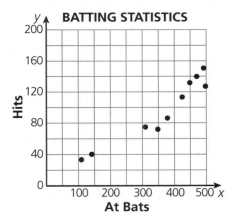

BATTING STATISTICS

Hits

At Bats

If this baseball player is at bat 250 times his next season, what would be the expected number of hits he makes?

A 20   **C** 60

B 40   **D** 80

SAMPLE Tiffany drew the trend line shown on this scatter plot.

Is the trend line she drew reasonable? Explain.

Answer _____

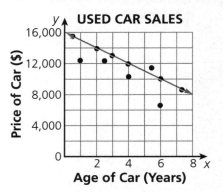

No, the trend line is not reasonable even though the line touches more than half the points on the scatter plot. A trend line should show the approximate pattern of the data points, with the distance of the points above the line equaling the distance of the points below the line.

Use the graph at the right to answer questions 3 and 4.

3 Roger made this scatter plot with trend line to show the relationship between the salaries of each employee at his company and the number of years each person was employed.

What does the *y*-intercept of the trend line represent?

Answer _____

_____

4 What does the slope of the trend line represent?

Answer _____

5 This scatter plot shows the relationship between the number of people in each group dining at a restaurant and the total amount of their dinner bill.

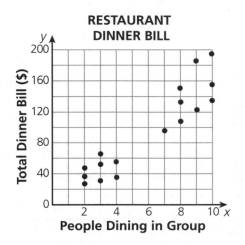

RESTAURANT DINNER BILL

Part A Draw a trend line on the scatter plot above that best fits the data points.

Part B Gayle used the equation $y = 20x$ to predict the total dinner bill for a group of 6 people. Use your trend line to explain whether or not this equation is a good fit for the data in the scatter plot.

What is the value of y in the equation when $x = 6$? Does this match the value shown on your trend line?

_____

_____

_____

_____

Two-Way Tables

8.SP.4

One variable of data in a two-way table is displayed in rows. The other variable is displayed in columns.

Frequency measures how many times, or how often, something occurs.

Look for patterns or trends in a table to help make conclusions.

To construct a two-way table, identify the two variables that represent the related pieces of data. One variable will represent rows of data. The other will represent columns of data.

A **two-way table** is a table that shows the **frequency,** or count, of two pieces of data. Two-way tables can be used to analyze data and make conclusions.

This table shows the salary ranges of each employee in different job classes at a company.

	Job Class		
Salary Range	**A**	**B**	**C**
$0–$25,000	0	11	58
$25,001–$50,000	10	41	22
$50,001–$100,000	44	48	0
$100,001+	16	0	0

A new employee will join the company with a starting salary of $23,850. What job class will this employee likely be in?

The data in this table shows employees with lower salaries tend to be in a higher letter job class. Most employees with salaries less than $25,000 are in job class C. So it is likely that this new employee will be in job class C.

Two-way tables can also be used to solve problems.

What fraction of all employees are in job class A and have salaries greater than $50,000?

Count the number of employees in job class A with salaries greater than $50,000: $44 + 16 = 60$

Count the total number of employees:

$$10 + 44 + 16 + 11 + 41 + 48 + 58 + 22 = 250$$

Write and simplify a fraction: $\frac{60}{250} = \frac{6}{25}$

So, $\frac{6}{25}$ of all the employees are in job class A and have salaries greater than $50,000.

SAMPLE In the school chorus, there are 9 sixth graders, 13 seventh graders, and 18 eighth graders. In the school orchestra, there are 6 sixth graders, 12 seventh graders, and 21 eighth graders. Which table shows this data?

A

	Chorus	Orchestra
Grade 6	6	9
Grade 7	7	13
Grade 8	8	18

C

	Chorus	Orchestra
Grade 6	9	6
Grade 7	13	12
Grade 8	18	21

B

	Chorus	Orchestra
Grade 6	6	15
Grade 7	7	25
Grade 8	8	39

D

	Chorus	Orchestra
Grade 6	9	15
Grade 7	13	25
Grade 8	18	39

The correct answer is C. In the table, the rows represent the grade level and the columns represent the school activity. The data in the first sentence goes under the column labeled "Chorus." The data in the second sentence goes under the column labeled "Orchestra."

1 This table shows the relationship between the number of house and condo listings for sale by one real-estate company and the number of bedrooms in each listing.

Bedrooms	Houses	Condos
1	3	17
2	8	16
3	18	5
4 or more	13	0

What fraction of the 2-bedroom listings are houses?

A $\frac{1}{8}$

C $\frac{1}{4}$

B $\frac{1}{6}$

D $\frac{1}{3}$

2 What is a reasonable conclusion that can be made from the data in the table?

Work Start Time (A.M.)	More than 7 Hours Sleep?	
	Yes	No
Before 7:00	5	19
7:00–8:00	12	11
After 8:00	20	23

A The workers starting after 8:00 get the most hours of sleep.

B About half of all workers get more than 7 hours of sleep each night.

C Most workers starting before 7:00 get less sleep than workers starting later.

D More than half of the workers starting after 8:00 get 8 hours of sleep.

SAMPLE This table shows the different dinner and dessert combinations chosen by guests at an awards dinner.

AWARDS DINNER

Dessert Choices	Dinner Choices			
	Fish	**Chicken**	**Beef**	**Eggplant**
Fruit Salad	15	18	6	5
Frozen Yogurt	12	15	24	4
Pudding	8	3	11	8

What fraction of the guests choosing chicken also had frozen yogurt?

Answer _____

First, count the total number of guests choosing chicken: 18 + 15 + 3 = 36. Of these, find the number of guests choosing frozen yogurt: 15. Divide this amount into the total to find the fraction: $\frac{15}{36} = \frac{5}{12}$. So, $\frac{5}{12}$ of guests choosing chicken also chose frozen yogurt.

3 A city bus company has a red line, a blue line, and a green line that travel different routes. Last month's arrival data for each route is listed below.

- The red line was early 21 times, on-time 64 times, and late 18 times.
- The blue line was early 15 times, on-time 84 times, and late 27 times.
- The green line was early 8 times, on-time 55 times, and late 22 times.

In the space below, create a two-way table to show the data.

© The Continental Press, Inc.   DUPLICATING THIS MATERIAL IS ILLEGAL.

4 The table below shows the results of a crash-test rating based on 5 stars for different types of vehicles. The higher the rating, the better the car performed in the test.

VEHICLE CRASH-TEST RATINGS

Vehicle Weight (lb)	Crash-Test Rating				
	1 ★	2 ★★	3 ★★★	4 ★★★★	5 ★★★★★
Less than 2,500	4	5	2	0	0
2,500–3,499	4	9	2	1	0
3,500–4,499	1	4	6	3	4
4,500+	0	0	2	4	9

Part A What fraction of the vehicles tested received less than 3 stars in the crash-test rating?

How many total vehicles were rated? How many of those vehicles received less than a 3-star rating?

Answer _____

Part B What conclusion can be made about the weight of a vehicle and the crash-test rating it received?

_____

_____

_____

REVIEW

Statistics and Probability

Read each problem. Circle the letter of the best answer.

1 Which scatter plot shows the best line of fit?

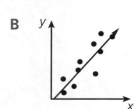

A

C

B

D

2 The equation $y = 1.6x + 2$ represents a trend line for this scatter plot.

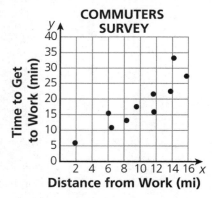

COMMUTERS SURVEY

Time to Get to Work (min)

Distance from Work (mi)

Based on this, what is the expected time it takes a commuter to travel 30 miles to work?

A   15 minutes   **C**   40 minutes

B   30 minutes   **D**   50 minutes

3 What can be concluded about mileage when weight increases?

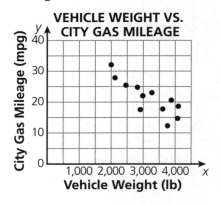

VEHICLE WEIGHT VS. CITY GAS MILEAGE

City Gas Mileage (mpg)

Vehicle Weight (lb)

A   Gas mileage tends to increase.

B   Gas mileage tends to decrease.

C   Gas mileage always increases.

D   Gas mileage always decreases.

4 What fraction of games won were soccer?

	Wins	Losses
Basketball	16	4
Soccer	10	5

A $\frac{2}{5}$ **C** $\frac{5}{9}$

B $\frac{5}{8}$ **D** $\frac{5}{13}$

5 This table shows the number of students in each foreign language class and how many are members of the international club.

Which class has the greatest percent of members in the international club?

Foreign Language Class	Member of International Club?	
	Yes	No
German	5	15
French	8	27
Italian	6	20
Spanish	8	36

Answer _____

6 This scatter plot shows the relationship between the time walked and the number of calories burned.

Based on this, how many calories would someone walking 60 minutes expect to burn?

CALORIES BURNED (WALKING)

Answer _____

7 Jack surveyed students in his school about the pets they have.

- Of the girls, 16 had dogs, 11 had cats, and 8 had no pets.
- Of the boys, 9 had dogs, 7 had cats, and 12 had no pets.

In the space below, create a two-way table to show the data.

8 This table shows the prices during a 40-year period for a first-class
postage stamp.

POSTAGE STAMP RATES

Year	Price (cents)
1971	8
1975	10
1981	20
1985	22
1991	29
1995	32
2001	34
2010	44

Part A On the coordinate plane below, draw a scatter plot to show
the data. Then draw a trend line on the scatter plot that best
fits the data.

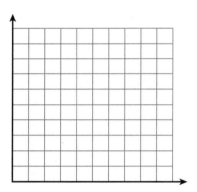

Part B What does the slope of the trend line you drew represent?

_____

_____

_____

UNIT 8 ▪▪
Statistics and Probability

PRACTICE TEST

1 What is the solution to the system of equations shown on this graph?

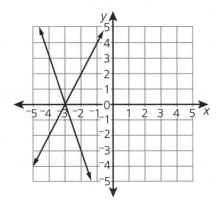

A (0, –3)   C (–3, 0)

B (–1, –3)   D (–3, –1)

2 What is the value of $\left(\dfrac{4^2}{4^{-1}}\right)^0$?

A 0   C 4

B 1   D 64

3 Which pair of figures shows a reflection?

A ▷◁   C ▷▷

B ▷◁   D ▷▷

4 Which function is **not** linear?

A $f(x) = 6 + x$ C $f(x) = 6 \cdot x$

B $f(x) = 6 - x$ D $f(x) = 6 \div x$

5 Which of the following is a rational number?

A 2π C 2.54769…

B $\sqrt{20}$ D $-\sqrt{\dfrac{3}{12}}$

6 Jacob asked students in his school whether they had a cell phone and an after-school job. The results are below.

Cell Phone?	After-School Job?	
	Yes	No
Yes	15	6
No	15	24

What fraction of the students Jacob asked have a cell phone?

A $\dfrac{1}{4}$ C $\dfrac{1}{2}$

B $\dfrac{7}{20}$ D $\dfrac{5}{7}$

7 Shan wrote the equation $n^2 = \dfrac{64}{100}$. What is the value of n?

A $\dfrac{4}{5}$ C $\dfrac{8}{25}$

B $\dfrac{16}{25}$ D $\dfrac{8}{50}$

8 This graph shows the total cost, y, for x pounds of dried fruit.

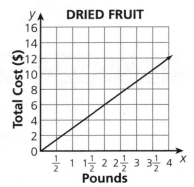

Which equation models this relationship?

A $y = \frac{1}{2}x$ **C** $y = 3x$

B $y = 2x$ **D** $y = 4x$

9 The diagram below shows the front view of a tent.

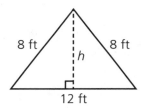

Which of the following measures is closest to the approximate height, h, of the tent?

A 5 ft   **C** 9 ft

B 6 ft   **D** 14 ft

10 Look at this system of equations.

$$\begin{cases} 3x - y = -6 \\ -2x - y = -4 \end{cases}$$

Is (-2, 0) a solution to this system of equations?

A Yes. It is a solution to both equations.

B No. It is not a solution to the first equation.

C No. It is not a solution to the second equation.

D No. It is not a solution to either equation.

11 Which decimal number **cannot** be written in fraction form?

A $-0.32\overline{9}$ **C** 2.16161…

B -0.8378   **D** 7.37342…

12 Which of the following represents the side lengths, in units, of an acute triangle?

A 2, 3, 4   **C** 6, 8, 9

B 2, 3, 5   **D** 6, 8, 10

13 Functions $f(x)$ and $g(x)$ are shown below.

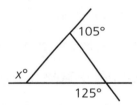

x	g(x)
-2	-1
-1	-3
0	-5
1	-7

Which statement best describes these functions?

A $f(x)$ and $g(x)$ are both linear.

B $f(x)$ and $g(x)$ are both nonlinear.

C $f(x)$ is linear and $g(x)$ is nonlinear.

D $f(x)$ is nonlinear and $g(x)$ is linear.

14 Look at this diagram.

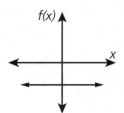

What is the value of x?

A 105   **C** 125

B 115   **D** 130

15 Which best describes the value of $\sqrt{2} + \pi$?

A less than 4

B between 4 and 5

C between 5 and 6

D greater than 6

16 What equation describes the function in this table?

x	0	1	2	3	4
y	10	8	6	4	2

A $y = 2x + 10$ **C** $y = -2x + 10$

B $y = 2x - 10$ **D** $y = -2x - 10$

17 Two transformations were performed on triangle PQR to get its image $P'Q'R'$ as shown on this coordinate plane.

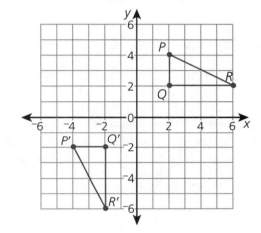

One transformation was a reflection across the x-axis. Which of the following describes the other transformation?

A 90° clockwise rotation about the origin

B 180° clockwise rotation about the origin

C 90° counterclockwise rotation about the origin

D 180° counterclockwise rotation about the origin

18 What is the approximate length of $\overline{FG}$ shown below?

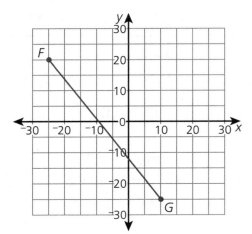

A 45 units

C 68 units

B 57 units

D 80 units

19 Figure *HIJK* is translated according to the rule $T_{-1,5}$ (*HIJK*) = *H'I'J'K'*. The coordinates of vertex *K* are (-6, -1). What are the coordinates of *K'*?

A (-7, 4)

C (-5, 4)

B (-7, -4)

D (-5, -4)

20 Figure 1 is transformed to make figure 2.

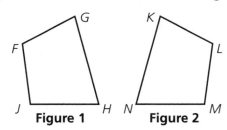

Which pair of angles must be congruent?

A ∠F and ∠K

C ∠H and ∠K

B ∠F and ∠M

D ∠H and ∠N

21 This scatter plot with line of best fit shows the relationship between the test price of a magazine subscription and the total number of subscriptions ordered.

What does the slope of this line represent?

A the cost per issue

B the change in the cost per issue

C the number of subscription orders

D the change in the number of orders as the cost increases

22 What is the solution to this equation?

$$4(m - 3) = 2(m - 4.5)$$

A $m = 0.75$

C $m = 1.5$

B $m = -0.75$

D $m = -1.5$

23 The total amount, *y*, a carpet company charges to install a carpet covering *x* square feet of space, including installation, is shown on this line graph.

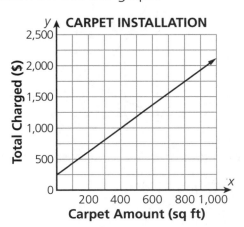

What does the *y*-intercept of this line represent?

A   the cost of the carpet

B   the cost of installation

C   the total amount charged

D   the total square feet of carpet

24 Which number is closest in value to *P* on the number line below?

A $\sqrt{20}$ **C** $\sqrt{40}$

B $\sqrt{30}$ **D** $\sqrt{60}$

25 A cone is 16 centimeters tall and has a diameter of 10 centimeters. What is the approximate volume of the cone?

A   419 cm^3 **C**   1,675 cm^3

B   1,256 cm^3 **D**   5,024 cm^3

26 Triangle *QRS* is dilated by a scale factor of *k* centered at the origin, as shown.

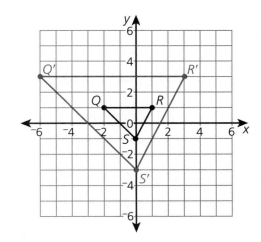

What is the value of *k*?

A $\frac{1}{3}$ **C** $\frac{3}{2}$

B $\frac{2}{3}$ **D** $\frac{3}{1}$

27 About 3.0×10^6 metric tons of cocoa are produced each year in the world. Of this, 1.5×10^5 metric tons are produced in Brazil. About how many metric tons of cocoa are produced in the rest of the world?

A 1.5×10^1 **C** 3.15×10^6

B 2.85×10^6 **D** 4.5×10^{11}

28 What is the solution to $\begin{cases} 5x - 2y = -1 \\ 2x - 3y = -7 \end{cases}$?

A   (1, 3)   **C**   (-1, -2)

B   (-3, 1)   **D**   (-2, -1)

29 Which statement best describes the graph of this function?

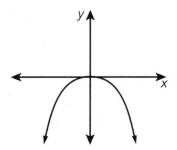

A   It increases for all values of *x*.

B   It decreases for all values of *x*.

C   It increases for positive values of *x* only.

D   It decreases for positive values of *x* only.

30 Similar triangles *PQS* and *RTS* are shown on this coordinate plane.

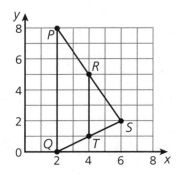

Which pair of sides has the same slope?

A $\overline{PQ}$ and $\overline{RT}$ only

B $\overline{PS}$ and $\overline{RS}$, and $\overline{QS}$ and $\overline{TS}$ only

C $\overline{PS}$ and $\overline{QS}$, and $\overline{RS}$ and $\overline{TS}$ only

D $\overline{PQ}$ and $\overline{RT}$, $\overline{PS}$ and $\overline{RS}$, and $\overline{QS}$ and $\overline{TS}$

31 How many solutions does this system of linear equations have?

$$\begin{cases} y = -2x + 1 \\ 4x + 2y = 2 \end{cases}$$

Answer _____

32 What function rule describes the pattern in this table used to get *y*?

x	2	4	8	16
y	6	8	12	20

Answer _____

33 Line *p* intersects lines *m* and *n,* as shown in this diagram.

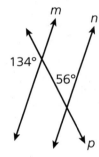

Are lines *m* and *n* parallel? Explain how you know.

_____

_____

_____

34 Are repeating and terminating decimals rational numbers? Explain how you know.

_____

_____

35 What is the input when the output is 10?

Input	0	1	2	3
Output	50	45	40	35

Answer _____

36 What is the value of the expression $\left(\frac{2^3 \cdot 2^{-5}}{2^{-4}}\right)^2$?

Answer _____

37 Figure 1 is transformed to make figure 2.

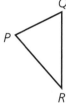 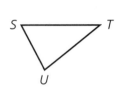

Figure 1   **Figure 2**

Which sides must be corresponding?

Answer _____

38 What value of w makes the equation $6w + 5 = 1$ true?

Answer _____

39 What is the solution to this system of equations? Show your work.

$$\begin{cases} 3x + y = 11 \\ x + 2y = 12 \end{cases}$$

Answer _____

40 The world's longest garden maze has a total path length of
approximately 12,989 feet. How is this number written in scientific
notation?

Answer _____

41 How many solutions are there to $5(z - 1) + z = 6z + 5$—
0, exactly 1, or more than 1?

Answer _____

42 Write a rational number that lies between $\sqrt{3}$ and π.

Answer _____

43 The graph and the table below show the relationship between the
weight and the total cost of two salads in a deli.

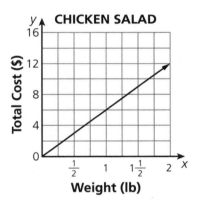

Weight (lb)	Total Cost ($)
$\frac{1}{4}$	2
$\frac{1}{2}$	4
$\frac{3}{4}$	6
1	8

TUNA SALAD

How does the cost per pound for each salad compare?

_____

_____

44 What is the measure of ∠L in the triangle below?

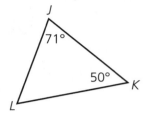

Answer _____

45 Between which two consecutive whole numbers is $\sqrt[3]{180}$?

Answer _____

46 This table shows the number of sweatshirts sold at a sporting goods store one day.

SWEATSHIRTS SOLD

	Gray	Blue
Small	6	6
Medium	16	12
Large	15	5

What fraction of sweatshirts sold were sized small?

Answer _____

47 The volume of this cylindrical canister is 50π cubic inches.

⊢ 5 in. ⊣

FLOUR

What is the height, in inches, of the canister?

Answer _____

48 Triangle *RST* is rotated 180° counterclockwise about point *R*.

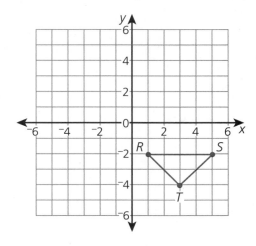

What are the coordinates of △*R'S'T'*, the image of △*RST*?

Answer _____

49 The triangle in the center of this diagram is a right triangle.

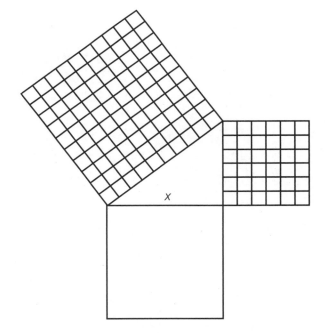

What is the length, in units, of the side of the triangle labeled *x*?
Explain how you know.

_____

_____

50 Lizzie drew line *k* on the coordinate plane below.

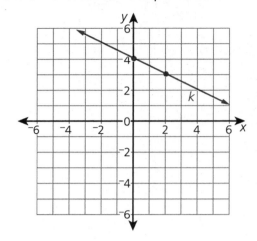

Write an equation in the form $y = mx + b$ that models line *k*.

Answer _____

Read the problem. Write your answer to each part.

51 John and Mario buy bags of dry pet food and cans of moist pet food. Each bag costs the same and each can costs the same.

- John pays $16.80 for 2 bags and 6 cans of pet food.
- Mario pays $14.00 for 1 bag and 10 cans of pet food.

Part A Write a system of equations that can be used to find the cost of each bag and the cost of each can of pet food.

Answer ______________________________

Part B Solve the system of equations you wrote in part A to find the cost of each bag and the cost of each can of pet food. Show your work.

Answer ______________________________

52 Lindsey studied 30 words as part of a memory test. She was then asked to remember as many words as possible at different periods of time. This table shows the results of this memory test.

MEMORY TEST RESULTS

Time (hours)	Words Remembered
1	27
2	22
4	23
8	15
12	14
20	12
24	10
30	10

Part A On the coordinate plane below, draw a scatter plot to show the data. Then draw a linear trend line on the scatter plot that best fits the data.

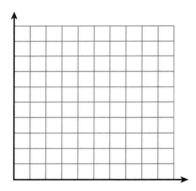

Part B What conclusion can be made from the data in the scatter plot you drew in part A?

_____

_____

_____

53 This rectangular prism has square bases.

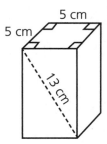

The length of the diagonal of the front side is 13 centimeters.

Part A What is the height, in centimeters, of this prism?

     Answer _____

Part B This prism is put inside a cylinder. What is the approximate volume, in cubic centimeters, of the smallest cylinder that this prism fits inside? Use 3.14 for π. Explain how you know.

_____

_____

_____

_____

GLOSSARY

acute triangle a triangle with all angles between 0° and 90°

additive inverse property states that if a number and its opposite are added, the sum is always 0: $a + (-a) = 0$

angle-angle similarity a way to show that two triangles are similar if two pairs of corresponding angles are congruent

base the number being multiplied in a number written in exponential form

center of dilation the point around which a figure is enlarged or reduced in a dilation

center of rotation the point around which a figure turns in a rotation

cluster a group of data points that are close together

commutative property allows numbers to be added or multiplied in any order, with the same sum or product: $a + b = b + a$ and $a \times b = b \times a$

cone a three-dimensional figure with a circular base and a curved side that meets at a point

congruent figures figures having the same size and shape; identical

constant a value that does not change, such as a unit rate

converse of the Pythagorean theorem states that if $a^2 + b^2 = c^2$, then there exists a right triangle with legs a and b and hypotenuse c

correlation a pattern that exists between two sets of data values in a scatter plot

corresponding matching

corresponding angles angles that are in the same position along a pair of lines

cubed	multiplied by itself twice
cube root	a number that is multiplied by itself twice, or cubed
cylinder	a three-dimensional figure with two circular bases and a curved side

D

dilation	a transformation that reduces or enlarges a figure
distance formula	a way to calculate the distance between two points on a coordinate plane. For any two points (x_1, y_1) and (x_2, y_2), the distance between them is $\sqrt{(x_1 - x_2)^2 + (y_1 - y_2)^2}$
distributive property	allows a number to be multiplied by a sum or each addend to be multiplied separately and the products added, with the same result: $a(b + c) = ab + ac$

E

elimination	a method for solving systems of equations algebraically by adding the equations together to eliminate one of the variables
ellipses	three periods (…) that indicate a number continues
equation	a number sentence that shows two expressions are equal
exponent	the number that shows how many times a number multiplies itself
exponential form	a number written as a number multiplied by itself several times
exterior angles	angles outside a set of lines or line segments

F

frequency	how often something happens, a count
function	a relationship between two sets of variables, called the input and the output. In a function, there is one unique output (y-value) for each input (x-value).
function notation	a way to write the equation of a function, in which x represents the inputs and $f(x)$ represents the outputs
function rule	a rule that describes the relationship between the input and output values of a function
function table	a table that represents a function as sets of ordered pairs

hypotenuse   the longest side of a right triangle, opposite the right angle

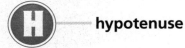

image   the resulting figure of the original figure after a transformation

improper fraction   a fraction with a numerator equal to or greater than the denominator

infinite   countless, unlimited

input   the *x*-values in a function

integers   whole numbers, including 0, and their opposites

interior angles   angles inside a set of lines or line segments

inverse operations   opposite operations that "undo" each other. Addition and subtraction are inverse operations. Multiplication and division are inverse operations.

irrational number   a real number that cannot be written in fraction form; a decimal that is non-terminating and non-repeating

laws of exponents   rules used to combine exponential expressions with the same base

legs   the two shorter sides of a right triangle, adjacent to the right angle

like terms   terms that have the same variable parts. Numbers without variable parts are also like terms.

linear function   a function that has the same change in *y*-values for each change in *x*-values. Its graph is a straight line.

linear relationship   a relationship that exists between the *x*- and *y*-values when data points in a scatter plot easily surround a straight line

line of best fit   a line that goes through data points on a scatter plot

line of reflection   the horizontal or vertical line over which a figure is flipped to create a reflection

nonlinear function a function that has varying changes in *x*- and *y*-values. Its graph is not a straight line.

nonlinear relationship a relationship that exists between the *x*- and *y*-values when data points in a scatter plot do not surround a straight line

non-repeating decimal a decimal number whose digits do not repeat

non-terminating decimal a decimal number whose digits do not end

obtuse triangle a triangle with exactly one angle between 90° and 180°

origin the center of a coordinate plane, located at the intersection of the *x*- and *y*-axes, having the coordinates (0, 0)

outlier a data value that is set apart from the rest

output the *y*-values of a function

parallel lines lines that do not intersect

perfect cube the product of the same three numbers

perfect square the product of a number and itself

pi an irrational number with a value of 3.1415926… that equals the ratio of the circumference of a circle to its diameter. An approximate value of pi is 3.14. The symbol for pi is π.

proportional relationship a relationship between two quantities in which the value of *x* always changes by a unit rate to produce *y*, represented as an equation of the form $y = ax$

Pythagorean theorem states that in a right triangle, the sum of the squares of the lengths of the legs, *a* and *b*, equals the square of the length of the hypotenuse, *c*: $a^2 + b^2 = c^2$

Pythagorean triple a set of whole number lengths of a right triangle

R

radical	a symbol, $\sqrt{}$, used to show a root; an expression that uses a radical sign
radicand	the number under a radical symbol
rational number	any number that can be written as a fraction, including whole numbers, integers, fractions, and some decimals
real numbers	the set of rational and irrational numbers
reflection	a transformation that flips a figure over a line to create a mirror image
repeating decimal	a decimal in which digits repeat in a pattern
right triangle	a triangle with exactly one 90°, or right, angle
rotation	a transformation that turns a figure around a point, either on or off the figure

S

scale factor	the factor by which each coordinate of a figure is multiplied to produce a dilation; the symbol for scale factor is k
scatter plot	a graph of plotted points that shows the relationship between two sets of data
scientific notation	a way of writing a number as a number greater than or equal to 1 and less than 10, multiplied by a power of 10
similar figures	figures have the same shape but proportional sizes
slope	the steepness of a line that shows how the change in one variable relates to the change in the other variable
slope-intercept form	one possible form of a linear equation: $y = mx + b$, in which m is slope and b is the y-intercept
solution	the value of a variable that makes an equation true
sphere	a three-dimensional figure made up of a set of points equidistant from a center point
squared	multiplied by itself
square root	the inverse of a perfect square

substitution	a method for solving systems of equations algebraically by rewriting one equation in terms of a single variable and then substituting the expression equal to that variable into the other equation
system of linear equations	a set of two or more linear equations

term	part of an expression or equation that is separated from others by addition or subtraction
terminating decimal	a decimal whose digits end
transformation	the movement of a geometric figure from one position to another
translation	a transformation that slides a figure from one place to another in a straight line
transversal	a line that intersects a pair of lines
trend line	an approximate line of best fit that is surrounded by the data points on a scatter plot and follows the general direction of the data
two-way table	a table that shows the frequency of two pieces of data

unit rate	a rate, or ratio, that compares a quantity to one unit

variable	a letter or symbol that represents an unknown value
vertical angles	angles opposite each other when a pair of lines intersects
volume	the amount of space inside a three-dimensional figure. Formulas for volume include

$$V_{cylinder} = \pi r^2 h \quad \text{a cylinder with radius } r \text{ and height } h$$

$$V_{cone} = \frac{1}{3}\pi r^2 h \quad \text{a cone with radius } r \text{ and height } h$$

$$V_{sphere} = \frac{4}{3}\pi r^3 \quad \text{a sphere with radius } r$$

 **x-axis**   the horizontal axis on a coordinate plane

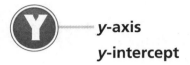 **y-axis**   the vertical axis on a coordinate plane

y-intercept   the point (0, b) where a line intersects the y-axis

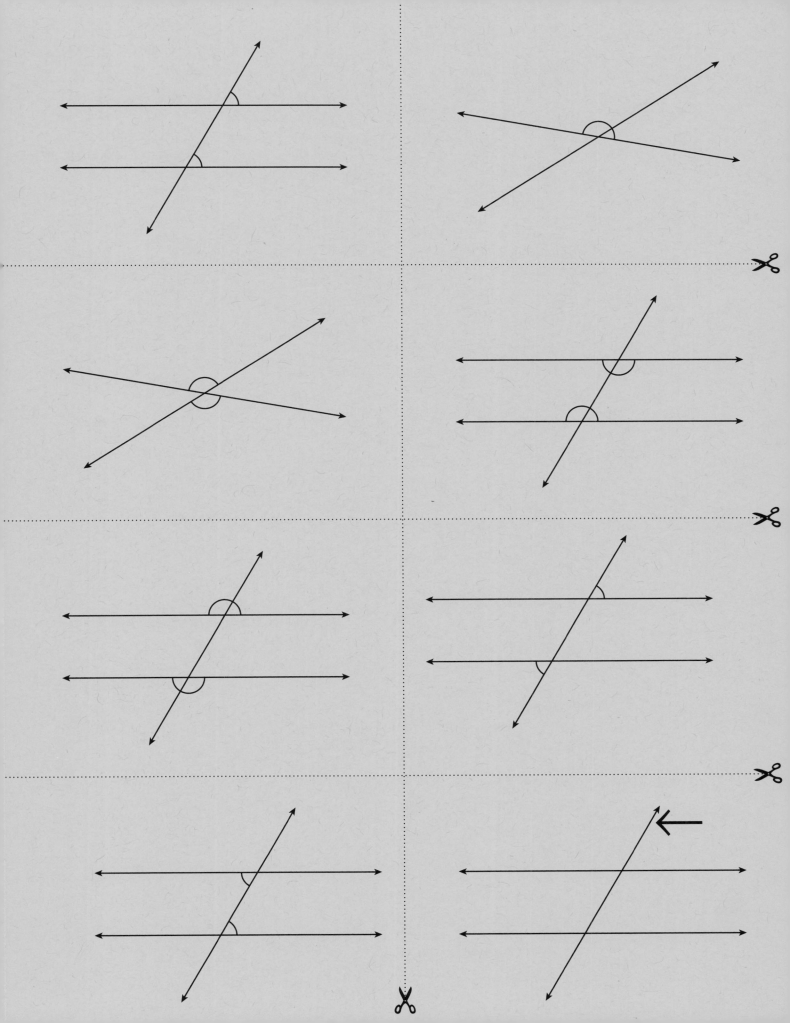

adjacent angles

corresponding angles

interior angles

vertical angles

alternate exterior angles

exterior angles

transversal

alternate interior angles

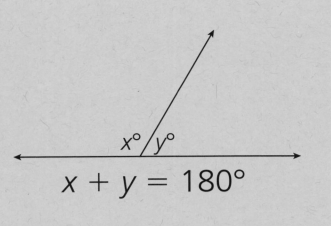

$x + y = 180°$

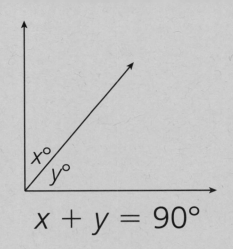

$x + y = 90°$

$\cong$

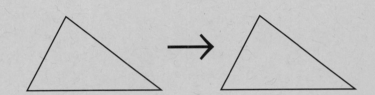

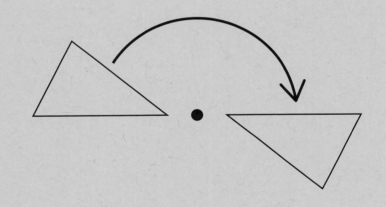

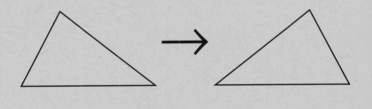

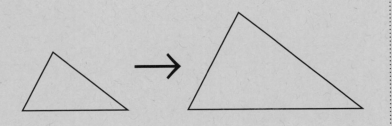

$y = mx + b$

complementary
angles

supplementary
angles

translation

is congruent to

reflection

rotation

slope-intercept form
m = slope
b = y-intercept

dilation

$y = ax^2 + bx + c$

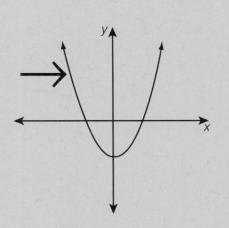

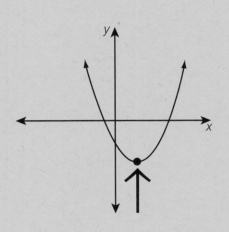

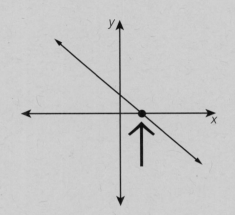

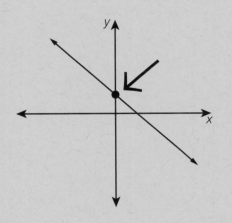

$$m = \frac{y_2 - y_1}{x_2 - x_1}$$

$180°(n - 2)$

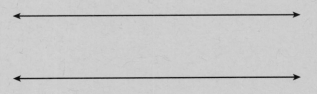

parabola

quadratic equation

x-intercept

vertex

slope formula

y-intercept

parallel lines

sum of measures
of interior angles
for any polygon